Peccadillo

A Comedy

by Garson Kanin

A SAMUEL FRENCH ACTING EDITION

FOUNDED 1830

SAMUELFRENCH.COM

Copyright © 1984, 1990 by T.F.T. Corporation

ALL RIGHTS RESERVED

CAUTION: Professionals and amateurs are hereby warned that *PECCADILLO* is subject to a licensing fee. It is fully protected under the copyright laws of the United States of America, the British Commonwealth, including Canada, and all other countries of the Copyright Union. All rights, including professional, amateur, motion picture, recitation, lecturing, public reading, radio broadcasting, television and the rights of translation into foreign languages are strictly reserved. In its present form the play is dedicated to the reading public only.

The amateur and professional live stage performance rights to *PECCADILLO* are controlled exclusively by Samuel French, Inc., and licensing arrangements and performance licenses must be secured well in advance of presentation. PLEASE NOTE that amateur licensing fees are set upon application in accordance with your producing circumstances. When applying for a licensing quotation and a performance license please give us the number of performances intended, dates of production, your seating capacity and admission fee. Licensing fees are payable one week before the opening performance of the play to Samuel French, Inc., at 45 W. 25th Street, New York, NY 10010.

Licensing fee of the required amount must be paid whether the play is presented for charity or gain and whether or not admission is charged.

Professional/Stock licensing fees quoted upon application to Samuel French, Inc.

For all other rights than those stipulated above, apply to: TFT Corporation, 210 Central Park South, #19D, New York, NY 10019.

Particular emphasis is laid on the question of amateur or professional readings, permission and terms for which must be secured in writing from Samuel French, Inc.

Copying from this book in whole or in part is strictly forbidden by law, and the right of performance is not transferable.

Whenever the play is produced the following notice must appear on all programs, printing and advertising for the play: "Produced by special arrangement with Samuel French, Inc."

Due authorship credit must be given on all programs, printing and advertising for the play.

ISBN 978-0-573-69188-1   Printed in U.S.A.   #18950

No one shall commit or authorize any act or omission by which the copyright of, or the right to copyright, this play may be impaired.

No one shall make any changes in this play for the purpose of production.

Publication of this play does not imply availability for performance. Both amateurs and professionals considering a production are strongly advised in their own interests to apply to Samuel French, Inc., for written permission before starting rehearsals, advertising, or booking a theatre.

No part of this book may be reproduced, stored in a retrieval system, or transmitted in any form, by any means, now known or yet to be invented, including mechanical, electronic, photocopying, recording, videotaping, or otherwise, without the prior written permission of the publisher.

MUSIC USE NOTE

Licensees are solely responsible for obtaining formal written permission from copyright owners to use copyrighted music in the performance of this play and are strongly cautioned to do so. If no such permission is obtained by the licensee, then the licensee must use only original music that the licensee owns and controls. Licensees are solely responsible and liable for all music clearances and shall indemnify the copyright owners of the play and their licensing agent, Samuel French, Inc., against any costs, expenses, losses and liabilities arising from the use of music by licensees.

IMPORTANT BILLING AND CREDIT REQUIREMENTS

All producers of *PECCADILLO must* give credit to the Author of the Play in all programs distributed in connection with performances of the Play, and in all instances in which the title of the Play appears for the purposes of advertising, publicizing or otherwise exploiting the Play and/or a production. The name of the Author *must* appear on a separate line on which no other name appears, immediately following the title and *must* appear in size of type not less than fifty percent of the size of the title type.

In addition the following credit *must* be given in all programs and publicity information distributed in association with this piece:

Original L.O.R.T. Production by
GEVA Theatre
Rochester, New York
Howard J. Millman, Producing Artistic Director
William B. Duncan, Managing Director

PECCADILLO premiered on March 12, 1985 at the Parker Playhouse in Ft. Lauderdale, under the aegis of Zev Bufman and Ivan Bloch; directed by Garson Kanin; with settings by Oliver Smith, costumes by Donald Brooks, lighting by Richard Nelson, and sound by Tony Meola ; with the following cast:

VITO DE ANGELIS	Christopher Plummer
ROBERT EPSTEIN	Todd Waring
RACHEL GARLAND DE ANGELIS	Glynis Johns
BRUCE	Tyrone Power
ERIC	John MacKay
IRIS PEABODY	Kelly McGillis
THE DOCTOR	Allen McCullough

PECCADILLO was subsequently presented at GeVa Theatre in Rochester, NY, Howard J. Millman, Producing Artistic Director, and William B. Duncan, Managing Director; directed by Stephen Rothman; with setting by Joseph Varga, costumes by Shigeru Yaji, lighting by Betsy Adams; and with the following cast:

VITO DE ANGELIS	Robert Strane
ROBERT EPSTEIN	Anthony Cummings
RACHEL GARLAND DE ANGELIS	Maeve McGuire
BRUCE	Bradford Wallace
ERIC	A. D. Cover
IRIS PEABODY	Elizabeth Dennehy

CHARACTERS

VITO DE ANGELIS – nearly 70, Italian, temperamental, handsome—a superb orchestral conductor

RACHEL GARLAND DE ANGELIS – over 50, but does not seem to have an age; a former opera star, now a perfect wife

ROBERT EPSTEIN – mid 30's, attractive, intelligent, a freelance writer

IRIS PEABODY – mid 20's, lovely and bright; an editor

ERIC)
)– the indispensable middle-aged servants
BRUCE)

TIME

1985

PLACE

The home of Mr. & Mrs. Vito De Angelis
Turtle Bay Gardens
New York, New York

ACT I

Scene 1	The study
April	Late afternoon
Scene 2	The sitting room
May	Early evening
Scene 3	The dining room
August	Midday

ACT II

Scene 1	The study
October	Afternoon
Scene 2	The sitting room
December	Morning
Scene 3	The dining room
April	Evening

The Author gratefully acknowledges the assistance of Romano Giachetti in preparing the Italian phrases used in the play.

To Marian Seldes with thanks,

And to Marian with love.

ACT I

Scene 1

As the HOUSE LIGHTS dim to darkness, we hear the sounds of a SYMPHONY ORCHESTRA tuning, warming up. Trills, runs, blasts, arpeggios, cadenzas.

A VOICE. Hold it! ... *Hold* it! (*SOUND subsides a few decibels. A BATON hits the metal stand on the podium, noisily.*) Quiet, please! ... Quiet!! (*The SOUND subsides, but not much. A BELL rings, to no effect.*) Sorry, Maestro. Best I can do.

THE POWERFUL VOICE OF VITO DE ANGELIS. *Ladies! Gentlemen! ... SHADDOP!!*

(*Instant silence.*)

FIRST VOICE. Thank you, Maestro ... Roll tape ... Take one. *Figaro Overture*. Houston Symphony. Conductor: Vito De Angelis.

(*All at once, the surrounding air is filled with the vibrant SOUND of a stirring performance of Mozart's Overture to The Marriage of Figaro.*
The stage is dark, except for a SPOTLIGHT on the CONDUCTOR leading the orchestra with enormous energy and style. We see only his expressive back and arms.

The MUSIC ends. APLAUSE. The SPOTLIGHT fades. LIGHTS come up on the study in the home of the conductor, Vito De Angelis.

Turtle Bay Gardens, New York City. A bright afternoon in April.

Throughout the play, the vital and varied New York City STREET SOUNDS will be heard.

You have doubtless heard of Maestro De Angelis. Even those indifferent to music know his name. He has seen to that. For in addition to being a superlative musician, his gifts extend to that greatest of all Twentieth Century Arts: Public Relations.

He never tells his age. He seems older to some, younger to others. Older to his wife of some 30 years, younger to his female adorers who find his undulating back, as he conducts, irresistibly sensuous.

The beautifully appointed study is a mosaic of certificates, plaques, signed photographs of musical greats, decorations, ribbons, medals, statuettes, gold records, honorary degrees, and assorted awards.

A Steinway grand piano. A $40,000 stereo installation. Part of one wall is a case holding thousands of records and cassettes and compact discs.

A plethora of mirrors, in which the Maestro studies and considers himself from time to often time.

The study is on the third floor of the five-story brownstone. Through the wide windows in the back wall can be seen the top of a tall elm tree.

VITO DE ANGELIS, The Maestro, is pacing about, slowly, while his literary ASSISTANT reads from a typescript on a portable Kluge desk on his lap. THE MAESTRO listens as he works on a lollipop. The assistant is ROBERT EPSTEIN, about 35, handsome, able, intelligent, humorous.)

ROBERT. (*Reading.*) "—and when an Argentinian interviewer asked, 'When did you begin to conduct?' I have replied, 'I have *always* conducted. So long as I can remember.' My father, who was concertmaster at La Scala in Milano for forty-four years, told me that at the age of three, I would stand in front of the phonograph—or the 'gramophone,' as it was then called— and conduct whatever music was playing.

(*THE MAESTRO, remembering, conducts in the manner of a small boy, smiling at himself in the nearest mirror.*)

ROBERT. My musical education, so, began at birth. In time, I became a fine pianist, an excellent cellist, and a superb clarinetist—but my big heart was always in conducting. Unfortunately, I was possessed of too much talent—

(*THE MAESTRO nods, gravely.*)

ROBERT. —and therefore, dangerous facility. Critics and rival conductors often sometime accused me of superficial preparation. At times, this may have been true, for I was always interested in life as well as in music. I wanted all that the good life has to offer—which is a very great deal." (*HE stops.*)—A great deal? A very great deal? No. A great deal. (*HE makes the correction.*)

(*THE MAESTRO, attempting to study his profile in a combination of two mirrors, remains oblivious to Robert's problem.*)

ROBERT. "Moreover, as I have often said—'Art should be what is left over from life.'"

VITO. (*Nods, sagely. In his charming Italian accent*) Beautyful. But was Sibelius say this, not me.

ROBERT. Oh? (*HE begins to rewrite.*)

VITO. No, no. Leave it. Sibelius, he don't care. Any*how*, who knows? (*HE laughs.*)

ROBERT. (*To the manuscript.*) Sorry, Jan. (*HE continues.*) "However, when Rachel Garland came into my life, I began to make full use of my God-given gifts. She provided the—"

VITO. "God-given gifts" *stinks*.

ROBERT. Pardon?

VITO. Guh guh guh. *God-given g*ifts. Ugly. Not musical.

ROBERT. But this isn't music, Maestro.

VITO. If is by me, must be musical. My public expects.

ROBERT. (*Frowns, thinking.*) God-given—uh—"talents?"

VITO. No.

ROBERT. "Art?"

VITO. No.

ROBERT. "Skill?"

VITO. *No.*

ROBERT. "Genius?"

VITO. (*Tempted.*) God-given genius. No. True, but no.

ROBERT. "Powers?"

VITO. No.

ROBERT. "Instinct?"

VITO. *No!*

ROBERT. "Propensity?"

VITO. Propensi—what?

ROBERT. How about "God-given gifts?"

VITO. God-given gifts. Ah! Good. You see? If is said correct, is musical. (*HE says it musically.*) God-given gifts.

ROBERT. (*Singing it to the first eight notes of Beethoven's Fifth Symphony.*) *God-giv-en-gifts! God-giv-en-gifts!*

VITO. Stop that! You know I hate such jokes. Desecrations.

ROBERT. Sorry.

VITO. Maestro.

ROBERT. Maestro.

VITO. You are too much some*time*, Robert, one smart *ass*.

ROBERT. Continue?

VITO. If you please. (*The Maestro, listening, begins to conduct the reading. We see why he is so dazzling on the podium. Fingers, hands, arms, torso—all give special meaning to the sound of the words.*)

ROBERT. "—I began to make full use of my—*God-given-gifts*. Rachel, she provided the inspiration which has led to aspiration. Up to that time, I sometimes traded on my flair, my platform charm, and my technical mastery. For a long time, I was able to fool the public. And as for the critics, well, what do they know of conducting? But when Rachel—"

VITO. Wait!

ROBERT. Yes?

VITO. Remove the critics. Is fine mans. Work hard. Hard job. I don't fight them. Never. Anyhow, I have not say that.

ROBERT. Yes, you did, Maestro. I have it right here in the transcript.

VITO. You have make a mistake.

ROBERT. "And as for the critics, well, what do they know of conducting?"

VITO. No.

ROBERT. I'll play you the tape.

VITO. To hell with your tape! Remove about the goddam know-nothing critics!

ROBERT. Very well. (*HE makes the cut in the manuscript.*) "For a long time I was able to fool the public. But when Rachel Garland has entered my life, all changed. She became, and has remained for so many unforgettable years, my partner, my helpmeet, my teacher, my friend."

VITO. (*Is weeping, softly.*) Beautiful! *Beautyful!*

ROBERT. Thank you.

VITO. (*Stops weeping.*) What "thank you?" *I* have said it, not *you*.

ROBERT. I put it down, Maestro. Edited it?

VITO. You break my *balls* with your goddam edit edit edit! You are pretty good secretary, but you don't know your place!!

ROBERT. I am *not* a secretary, Maestro. Mr. De Angelis.

VITO. Maestro.

ROBERT. I am your ghostwriter.

VITO. (*Looking about.*) Ghostwriter! Sshh! You know your contract? Confidential? Nothing to be said? Never?

ROBERT. You're a difficult man, Mr. De Angelis.

VITO. (*Automatically.*) Maestro.

ROBERT. And if I weren't so far into this ... Ten *months* I've put in, and they seem like twenty—I don't know.

(*VITO undergoes a sudden character shift. HE becomes all smiles, exuding charm.*)

VITO. Come on, Roberto. We have a drink. No?
ROBERT. No.
VITO. A martini. Yes?
ROBERT. Too early.

VITO. No fight, hey? We great together, no?
ROBERT. No, but— (*HE sits.*)
VITO. Come on.
ROBERT. All right.
VITO. Sure no drink?
ROBERT. Thank you, Maestro. No.
VITO. Maestro.
ROBERT. (*Takes up the manuscript again.*) "I met Rachel in Vienna, that most magically musical and ineffably romantic of cities ..."
VITO. (*Happily.*) My most favorite part! (*He catches a glimpse of himself in one of the mirrors. HE puffs his hair above his ears, squints, gets out a pair of eyeglasses and puts them on, the better to admire himself.*)
ROBERT. (*Continuing.*) "Musical because romantic, romantic because beautiful. It was a time when much light work was played for balance. I had agreed to conduct a New Year's Eve performance of Johann Strauss's glorious *Die Fledermaus*. Rare because how many works are light and great? *Die Fledermaus* expresses so exquisitely the Viennese temperament—described by von Hofmannsthal as,
VITO/ROBERT. (*Together.*) 'One eye wet; and the other dry.'
ROBERT. (*Continuing.*) At the first rehearsal, from the very first note she sang—Rachel she has owned my heart. She had come over from the Metropolitan to sing Adele, the lovely little maid, and she sang it better than it had ever been sung before—or since. I wooed her, but with no success. She had, alas, heard of my reputation as a womanizer and—"
VITO. No good! "Womanizer" no good.
ROBERT. Why not?
VITO. Sounds dirty.
ROBERT. It's not, though.

VITO. But *sounds!* All what matters is *sounds!*
ROBERT. "—as a Don Juan—?"
VITO. No. Boring part, Don Giovanni.
ROBERT. "—as a Casanova—?"
VITO. "—as a Casa—" No.
ROBERT. "—as a Lothario—?"
VITO. —a gigolo!
ROBERT. "—as a gall*ant*—?"
VITO. Too French.
ROBERT. "—as an amorist—?"
VITO. Is such a word?
ROBERT. Yes.
VITO. No. Sounds political. The Amorist Party.
ROBERT. "—as a ladies' man—?"
VITO. Buono! Nice. Is polite? Chic?
ROBERT. Oh, yes.
VITO. (*Pointing to the manuscript.*) Put.

ROBERT. (*Makes the revision.*) "But I have persisted, because I knew that she was the rest of me. It took more than one year, but then at last, in December, nineteen-fifty-nine, we became the man and wife. I had not intended to marry, never. After all, I was almost forty and had—"

VITO. Take out "almost forty." Is nobody's business.

ROBERT. Just say "thirty-eight?"

VITO. Just say nothing, goddammit! What are you writing—I mean what I am writing—some kind arithmetics book?

ROBERT. (*Working on the manuscript.*) "After all, I was a confirmed bachelor and had been all my life."

VITO. Take out "confirmed."

ROBERT. Why?

VITO. Sounds religious.

ROBERT. Oh, for the love of—! (*He stops, resigned, and makes the cut.*) "After all I was a bachelor and had been all my life. But as my friend Pablo Picasso once said to me: 'Vito, it takes a long time to become young!'"

VITO. Good!

ROBERT. (*Continuing.*) "In Naples, where—"

VITO. In *beautyful* Naples.

ROBERT. But it's *not* beautiful.

VITO. To me, *yes!* Is my book, my city, so say beautyful.

ROBERT. But if—

VITO. Say beautyful beautyful Naples.

ROBERT. Beautyful beautyful?

VITO. Beautyful beautyful!

ROBERT. (*Sotto voce, as HE enters it.*) Boy, *you're* beautyful!

VITO. What do you say?

ROBERT. I say beautyful beautyful.

VITO. Continue.

ROBERT. "After all, I was a bachelor and had been all my life! (*Gagging on the next.*) In beautyful beautyful Naples where I was born, is an old saying:

ROBERT and VITO. 'Uno scapolo è un uomo che non commette mai lo stesso errore una volta sola.'

ROBERT. 'A bachelor is a man who never makes the same mistake once.'"

VITO. (*Laughs heartily.*) Buono, yes?

ROBERT. No.

VITO. (*In two syllables.*) *No*-o? ... Why no?

ROBERT. Stale.

VITO. What means "stale?"

ROBERT. È vecchia!

VITO. È vecchia! *You* are vecchio.

(*ROBERT rises.*)

VITO. Sorry.

(*ROBERT sits.*)

VITO. Continue. Please.
ROBERT. (*Pressing on, doggedly.*) "After our marriage, Rachel *insisted* upon giving up her career at once, so as to be able to remain at my side to help me. I have begged her not to do so. 'You must have self-expression,' I have said. And she has said, '*You* will be my self-expression.' Life began."
VITO. Bravo!

(*HE applauds, and takes off his glasses. ROBERT is about to speak, but does not. VITO goes to the house intercom, presses a button.*)

A VOICE. Yes, Maestro?
VITO. Eric! Bruce! We have the tea, please. (*To Robert.*) So. How much more, you think?
ROBERT. I'd say we're a touch more than halfway through.
VITO. That is all?

(*ROBERT shrugs.*)

VITO. So ... ten months more?
ROBERT. Oh, God, no! Remember, six of the first ten were talking and taping and transcribing. No, I'd say another three months for the first draft, and maybe a month to polish.
VITO. (*Looking through a gold date book.*) So the polish month—it will be hard because I am in Chicago, Detroit, Houston, Los Angeles.
ROBERT. Have pen, will travel.
VITO. What?

(*A KNOCK. ERIC and BRUCE, the attractive, beige-jacketed servants, wheel in a well-stocked tea table. They are followed by RACHEL, a beguiling creature of indeterminate age, who goes at once to Vito. THEY kiss a long married kiss, more cheeks than lips.*)

RACHEL. Darling.
VITO. Cara mia.

(*SHE goes to ROBERT, and THEY shake hands.*)

RACHEL. Bobby.
ROBERT. Hello.
RACHEL. And how did it go today, dear laborers? (*Her voice is musical, her presence magical. Men fall in love with her straightaway, women wish to be her.*)
ROBERT and VITO. (*Together.*) Fair/ Excellent!
RACHEL. I *did* hear *some* screaming. Key of G-major.
ROBERT. It was nothing.
VITO. A small misunderstanding. Poco poco. You rather a drink, Bob?
ROBERT. No, thank you. I have to work tonight.
VITO. Robert—is so good that sometime one word—small, not important—but stands out because wrong. Like one wrong note.
ROBERT. (*To Rachel.*) And that *ear* of his!
RACHEL. Which one?

(*THEY laugh together. VITO does not get it. RACHEL gives Vito his tea.*)

VITO. Grazie.(*HE begins to leaf through his copy of the manuscript.*)
RACHEL. Where have we got to?

ROBERT. Today, he finally got you to say yes.
RACHEL. To what?
ROBERT. To marriage.
RACHEL. Oh, *that* yes. Nineteen-fifty-nine. It certainly doesn't *seem* like only yesterday.
VITO. (*Looking at the manuscript.*) You know, some*time* I think in this, the English is not too the best.
ROBERT. That is quite intentional, Maestro.
VITO. Why *is?*

(*ROBERT and RACHEL exchange a look.*)

RACHEL. Did you read those reviews on Domingo this morning?
VITO. (*To Robert.*) Why is?
ROBERT. (*To Rachel.*) Are they good?
RACHEL. Stupendous.
VITO. Why *is?*
RACHEL. Your needle seems to be stuck, darling.
VITO. Why *is?*
ROBERT. Why is *what*, Maestro? I've forgotten the subject.
VITO. Why it is quite intentional the not so best English?
ROBERT. (*Takes a deep breath.*) Because, Maestro, as I understand it—Little, Brown is anxious to make it appear that this is not a "*with* so and so," not "as told to," not a collaboration—but simply—(*He places it in the air.*)—MAESTRO by Vito De Angelis.
VITO. So?
ROBERT. So as I perceive my duties and responsibilities—I am to try to write it as *you* would write it, as if in the case you would be yourself the writing down.
VITO. Which means?

ROBERT. Which means I make a kind of charming patois and then we inside to out so all will think was you you you you *you!*

VITO. Bad English?

ROBERT. Not bad. Different. Personality. Image.

VITO. I am some Mulberry Street dago?

RACHEL. Vito!

VITO. (*With an imperious gesture.*) Out! I am fire you!

ROBERT. Good! I am quit!

RACHEL. Please, boys.

VITO. Out! Out!

RACHEL. Vito! Bobby!

ROBERT. (*Getting his things.*) No way, lady! I've taken all I'm going to take. Ten months of this egomaniac.

VITO. Idiot! Know-nothing! Pederast! Faggot! (*To Rachel.*) Qu'est-ce qu-on dit "salaud?"

RACHEL. Son of a bitch.

VITO. Son of a bitch.

(*BRUCE comes in.*)

ROBERT. Up yours, Maestro!
VITO. Come si dice bastardo? Presto! Presto!
RACHEL. Bastard.
VITO. *Bastard.*

(*Now a stream of gutter invective in several languages. VITO's voice reaches a high pitch. HE is apoplectic. HE throws his cup at Robert, misses. BRUCE catches it, and exits. HE puts on his eyeglasses and throws a plate. ROBERT ducks and moves away. The teapot. Almost. ROBERT is considering belting this madman. RACHEL catches his eye and motions him out of the room. As a matter of safety, HE backs out, using his*

Kluge desk as a shield against further flying objects. VITO pauses for breath.)

ROBERT. *(At the door.)* Maestro—you can *kiss* mine!
VITO. *(At his peak.)* Is too *late* to apologize! Out!

(ROBERT and RACHEL look at each other. No use. THEY cannot help bursting into laughter. VITO, confused, is breathing hard.
The LIGHTS dim swiftly.
In the darkness we hear the great recording of Die Fledermaus. Rachel Garland is singing—in English— Adele's celebrated laughing song.)

ACT I

Scene 2

The LIGHTS come up. The MUSIC fades. We are in the living room. It is an enchanting place, clearly untouched by professional interior decoration. Instead, it reflects the combined personalities of Rachel and The Maestro. A comfortable, utilitarian, warm, lived-in space.
In the background, as always in this house, MUSIC is playing, softly. At the moment, it is a recording of Kinderscenen by Schumann.
A large, superb Grandma Moses, which hangs over the fireplace, seems to have been painted there by the artist. A Reginald Marsh burlesque nude. A Horace Pippin. These are Rachel's pictures. The Maestro's are: a grand Canaletto, an exquisite Raphael (yes!), a Caravaggio,

and the famous Picasso portrait of The Maestro on the podium, lighted dramatically.

The furniture, too, combines New England and Italian modern. Plants and fresh flowers abound—the latter stunningly arranged by Rachel.

The living room is on the second floor. Through the window, we see the elm again, this time its trunk.

Upstage, the large double doors set in the archway lead to the hall and the curved staircase.

From time to time, when the doors are open, we see BRUCE or ERIC or both going about their household duties. In this scene, their jackets are maroon.

A month has passed. It is now May. Early evening.

RACHEL and a YOUNG WOMAN, both standing, are in the midst of a tense, acrimonious argument. The young woman is IRIS PEABODY, a senior editor representing the staid and illustrious Boston publishing firm of Little, Brown and Company. She is shapely and leggy. Her hair is piled high on her splendid head, revealing an exceptional neck. She is handsome rather than pretty and projects a magnetic vitality. She wears eyeglasses which accentuate her beauty.

RACHEL and IRIS have reached that point in debate where both adversaries are talking at the same time.

IRIS.	RACHEL.
—simply will not postpone for a *third time!* It's making us look ridiculous in the eyes of the publishing world, and what's more—	Why not? What is so impossible about a postponement?

(THEY stop together, momentarily exhausted.)

IRIS. I did *not* say, Mrs. De Angelis, that a postponement was impossible. I said that Little, Brown is not *prepared* to postpone for a third time.

RACHEL. But what's the alternative?

IRIS. Call it off.

RACHEL. (*Astounded.*) Call it *off*?

IRIS. Take it elsewhere. You may find a publisher with more patience, although I doubt it.

RACHEL. Do you mean to tell me that your company is willing to give up this remarkable piece of—

IRIS. It isn't a remarkable *anything*, Mrs. De Angelis. Not yet.

RACHEL. It's half done.

IRIS. We can't sell half a book.

RACHEL. But you—

IRIS. Could he sell half a *recording*?

RACHEL. Oh, don't talk nonsense!

IRIS. Sorry, I suppose that was. But here's something that's not.

(*SHE takes a folder out of her Gucci envelope and extracts a single sheet. SHE goes on talking, but RACHEL never takes her eyes off that sheet.*)

IRIS. Our comptroller sent this up to the Board last week. Then the publisher sent for me. All *my* fault, of course. I should have seen to it that—. Why didn't I—? The fact that I haven't been personally involved—that Mr. De Angelis's editor kept assuring me that—

RACHEL. What does it say?

IRIS. —what say?

RACHEL. That.

IRIS. (*Looking at it.*) The comptroller estimates that thus far, the De Angelis deal has cost us more than sixty-six thousand dollars in non-recoverable monies, over and above the advance.

RACHEL. I don't understand how it—

IRIS. The contract for this book was signed four years ago—

RACHEL. It *couldn't* be.

IRIS. (*Consults the sheet.*) Four years, less six weeks. At that time, the due date was fixed at one year from signing.

RACHEL. But that turned out to be an exceptionally busy year for him: La Scala to Covent Garden to San Francisco to Chicago to—

IRIS. Spare me. I'm getting jet lag.

RACHEL. Busy, don't you see?

IRIS. (*Consults the paper again.*) At any rate, the comptroller tells us that the expenses and interest on this amount—comes to sixty-six thousand, seven-hundred-eight dollars and sixty-four cents.

RACHEL. But what do you want us to do?

IRIS. It's not a question of what *I* want to do. I'm not an "I." I'm only a messenger. I hate this chore. Because I find I like *you.*

RACHEL. Thank you.

IRIS. And as for *Mr.* De Angelis—

RACHEL. (*Automatically.*) The Maestro.

IRIS. And as for The Maestro—I've been a besotted fan for years. And even though I've never met him—I didn't want to, really. It would be like meeting Chopin or Dickens or DaVinci—I've admired him more than I can say.

RACHEL. Does that mean you don't admire him *now?*

IRIS. (*A pause.*) Our present position is this. We wish to cancel our contract for the book tentatively titled MAESTRO by Vito De Angelis, and The Maestro is to return to us immediately the sum of one hundred and eighty-three thousand seven hundred and eight dollars and sixty-four cents.

(*During the above, RACHEL gets up and goes to the door. But instead of of leaving, SHE closes it and returns to the scene.*)

RACHEL. Miss Peabody, in the circumstances, it is now necessary to tell you something.
IRIS. Yes?
RACHEL. The Maestro does have seven hundred and eight dollars. And sixty-four cents.
IRIS. I'm sure of it.
RACHEL. What he does not have is the hundred-and-eighty-three thousand.
IRIS. (*Looking around.*) None of my business, but I'd say these pictures are worth what used to be called "a pretty penny."
RACHEL. The American ones are *mine*.
IRIS. Oh.
RACHEL. And the Italian ones have been *loaned* to him by various friends and admirers: Norton Simon, William Paley, Mary Lasker.
IRIS. I see. (*IRIS is looking around again.*)
RACHEL. The house? Mine. And everything in it, except, of course *his* things: the piano, scores, stereo, clothing. He does have terribly expensive clothing—but I don't think one hundred, eight-three thousand dollars worth.
IRIS. Mrs. De Angelis, what do you expect *us* to do? Have you any suggestions?
RACHEL. Wait. You'll get your book. We must *find* a writer.
IRIS. We've now had *five*—do you realize that? —five in four years! (*SHE gets out another sheet.*) Fred Myers—

RACHEL. Yes, I remember. Bald-headed. Refused to fly. So how he could stay with The Maestro and continue to—?

IRIS. Barbara Weeks—an excellent ghost who's done six of the best—

RACHEL. Fifty-five years old and made a pass at him one night.

IRIS. Oh? (*HER eyebrows go up and SHE gives her head a single shake to clear it of this information.*) Charles Fredericks?

RACHEL. Thirty-five years old and made a pass at him one night.

IRIS. (*Gulps.*) Don't tell me Anne *McKay* made a pass at him. She's the most straight-laced young—

RACHEL. With her, it was the other way about.

IRIS. Oh, dear.

RACHEL. And her husband objected.

IRIS. And then—Robert Epstein.

RACHEL. Oh, yes. Bobby.

IRIS. One of the best writers I know. Not really a ghost. I was astonished when he accepted the assignment.

RACHEL. He loved The Maestro, that's why.

IRIS. And the chapters he turned in are—well, superlative.

RACHEL. But they quarreled. Made up, quarreled again. On and off and finally—off, for good.

IRIS. Do you think there's a chance they might—?

RACHEL. No, no. Out of the question.

IRIS. Well, then. There we are.

RACHEL. There *must* be someone!

IRIS. Shall we get in touch with your lawyer? Or with his agent? Is it still Irving Paul Lazar?

(*Suddenly, RACHEL smiles a bright, radiant, happy, relaxed smile. In the silence, her thoughts become crystal clear.*)

IRIS. Oh, *no!* (*SHE gets up and begins to collect her things.*)
RACHEL. Just a moment—
IRIS. No lion's den for me, thank you.
RACHEL. How badly do you want this book finished?
IRIS. Not *that* badly.
RACHEL. Would you try for a few days?
IRIS. No!
RACHEL. For one day?

(*RACHEL is hypnotizing, casting a spell. IRIS shakes her head.*)

IRIS. (*A whisper.*) No, thank you.
RACHEL. For an hour. Fifteen minutes? Five?
IRIS. It's no use, Mrs. De Angelis. I couldn't. Even if I could, I wouldn't.
RACHEL. But why not?
IRIS. Terrified.
RACHEL. Sit down.
IRIS. No.
RACHEL. For a moment.

(*As RACHEL goes to the intercom, IRIS moves to the farthest corner of the room as if to hide.*)

VITO'S VOICE. Si.
RACHEL. (*On the intercom.*) Vieni giù, caro mio ...È importante, credimi ... No, solo la ragazza di Little, Brown. È un guaio ... Un grosso guaio. Vogliono il libro o rivogliono il denaro.

VITO'S VOICE. (*Explosively.*) Il *denaro!!*

(*RACHEL pulls the phone away from her ear, as it screeches hysterically. SHE looks up at Iris and smiles. SHE returns to the phone, weakly.*)

RACHEL. Sì, hai ragione. Ma ho una soluzione, credo ... vieni giù e ne parliamo ... (*To Iris.*) He'll be right down.

(*IRIS, in a panic, picks up her things, preparatory to making a swift exit.*)

IRIS. Mrs. De Angelis, I live in Boston, where I have a good life and a good job. And a splendid young man who–. (*Distracted.*) And I'm not in a position to leave all that— even for a short time— to, well, to produce—help to—.
RACHEL. It wouldn't take long. A few weeks. I'd want you to come and stay here, with us, of course.
IRIS. What?
RACHEL. The food is excellent. The guest room is comfortable. (*SHE smiles.*) And the price is right.
IRIS. My boss wouldn't—
RACHEL. I'll take care of that. (*Indicating the door.*) Or *he* will.

(*VITO comes charging into the room. HE goes at once to the bar tray to fix a drink. HE and IRIS are on opposite sides of the room. RACHEL stands between them. An oppressive silence. HE knocks back a vodka and turns into the room.*)

VITO. Now. What is this sheet about give back monies?
RACHEL. Vito!

VITO. I don' ask you. I ask him.
RACHEL. He is a woman.
VITO. So? I ask she.
IRIS. Maestro, with all due respect—
VITO. I don' give it back money. Never!!
RACHEL. (*To Iris.*) Let me explain, would you?
IRIS. By all means.
VITO. No! (*To Rachel.*) Out!
RACHEL. What?
VITO. Business. I take care.
RACHEL. But, darling, I told you. I had a —
VITO. (*Fortissimo.*) Vattene. Vattene via! O ti spacco la testa.
RACHEL. (*Smiles at Iris.*) Good luck, dear.

(*SHE goes. VITO squints across the room at Iris.*)

IRIS. You see, Maestro, the problem is—
VITO. Is *what?*
IRIS. We haven't received the manuscript.
VITO. *Your* fault!
IRIS. Ours?
VITO. Of course, ours—because you send me to help only idiots, cretins, fairies, nymphomaniacs!
IRIS. (*Angrily.*) They weren't when they arrived here, Maestro. They may have been by the time they left.

(*VITO is astonished. People simply do not speak to The Maestro in this way. HE squints across the room. Now HE reaches into his pocket and takes out his eyeglasses. As HE puts them on, IRIS quickly takes hers off. HE looks at her. A long moment, during which a police car speeds by on Second Avenue, emitting that nerve-testing HiLo siren wheep! wheep! wheep! wheep! SOUND. VITO metamorphoses into another human being, takes a step toward her. Now HE smiles, charmingly.)*

VITO. (*Gently.*) So. You are a Little Brown.
IRIS. No. I'm Iris.
VITO. Yes. You look it.
IRIS. What?
VITO. You *look* Irish. What is your name?
IRIS. Peabody.
VITO. Peabody what?
IRIS. (*Confused.*) Peabody Irish ... Irish Peabody ... Iris.
VITO. You are the one she wants me give back money?
IRIS. No, I'd rather have the book.
VITO. I give it to you. O.K.?
IRIS. I mean the *whole* book.
VITO. Sure. But I need the help.
IRIS. I know.
VITO. All those ones, may*be* good peoples, but not—how you say in English "simpatico?"
IRIS. You say "simpatico."
VITO. Is a English word?
IRIS. Yes.
VITO. I bet you wrong.
IRIS. You'll lose.
VITO. You are one expert, eh?
IRIS. Yes.
VITO. You know what else more?
IRIS. I'm afraid so.
VITO. Simpatico. I can tell. Is my talent. I know in uno momento. I meet the soloist. "How do you do?" "How do you do, Maestro?" Shake the hand. (*He pantomimes the action.*) And I know. Is he possible? Is he professional? Or prick? Same with you. I can tell. You are professional. No prick.

IRIS. No. None at all.
VITO. What?
IRIS. (*Madly befuddled.*) I don't know.
VITO. No capito. You speak maybe Italian?
IRIS. No. And right now, I'm not so sure I speak maybe English.
VITO. You speak nice English.
IRIS. Thank you.
VITO. You are musical?
IRIS. I think so. I play the piano. Badly.
VITO. Never let me hear you!
IRIS. No sir.
VITO. Maestro.
IRIS. Maestro.
VITO. You have seen me conduct?
IRIS. Oh, yes. many times.

(*VITO waits.*)

VITO. Go on.
IRIS. You're magnificent.
VITO. I know.
IRIS. My favorite. An idol, really.
VITO. Thank you.
IRIS. That's why I suggested the book.
VITO. *You* suggest?
IRIS. Yes, of course.
VITO. Maestro.
IRIS. Maestro.
VITO. *You* suggest and now *you* want back money?
IRIS. (*In a daze.*) I don't want anything.
VITO. Sit.

(*SHE does so.*)

VITO. You are writer?
IRIS. Editor.
VITO. But you can write?
IRIS. I think so.
VITO. I make you martini? Yes? (*He starts for the bar tray.*)
IRIS. Yes.

(*VITO stops.*)

IRIS. Maestro.
VITO. (*Continues to the bar tray and prepares martinis. A ritual.*) Where you live?
IRIS. Boston.
VITO. Massachusetts?
IRIS. Yes.
VITO. Too far.
IRIS. Yes.
VITO. But excellent string section, The Boston. Maybe best.
IRIS. Thank you.
VITO. How old?
IRIS. The Boston Symphony?
VITO. No, you.
IRIS. Twenty-seven.
VITO. True?
IRIS. No?
VITO. How much?
IRIS. Twenty-five.
VITO. (*Laughing.*) You are astonishment.
IRIS. I am?
VITO. In each country—always—the woman—they lie of the age—but always the *less*—not the *more* as you.
IRIS. How old are *you?*
VITO. What?!

IRIS. How old are *you?*
VITO. I am *not* old. I am *young*.
IRIS. Never mind. I'll look you up in *Who's Who*.
VITO. No true *Who Who*.
IRIS. I'll ask your wife.
VITO. She don' know.
IRIS. No matter. I'm not really interested.
VITO. You would be amaze!
IRIS. I'm sure of it.

(*HE comes to her. SHE stands. HE hands her a martini, and notices that she is a bit taller than he. HE stretches and plays the rest of the scene on tiptoe, more or less.*)

VITO. You are married?
IRIS. No.
VITO. Divorced?
IRIS. No.
VITO. You have not been married? Never? Twenty-five?
IRIS. Never.
VITO. You are lesbian?
IRIS. Not yet, no.
VITO. Why you don' marry?
IRIS. I don't believe in it.
VITO. *Why* you don'?
IRIS. It's unnatural. Marriage isn't nature's idea—it never was. It's man's.
VITO. You sure you twenty-five, not seventy-five?
IRIS. Do you know what the natural function of the human female is?
VITO. (*Beaming.*) Oh, yes.
IRIS. It's to become impregnated and reproduce as often as physically possible.
VITO. (*Crosses himself.*) Per carita!

IRIS. And the male is supposed to go around impregnating as many females as he possibly can.

VITO. (*Smiling proudly.*) I will do my best.

IRIS. That's the *natural* law. And what does that have to do with marriage?

VITO. You are crazy and charming, Irish. So when we begin?

IRIS. Begin what?

VITO. My book. Begin to finish.

IRIS. I don't think Little, Brown would—

VITO. I take care. So. Fine?

IRIS. No. I've decided. No.

(*HE comes to her, takes her hand, kisses it Italian style, and still holding it, smiles a Neapolitan smile.*)

VITO. Hey! What kind a ring this?

IRIS. My engagement ring.

VITO. You say you don' marry.

IRIS. I don't. I won't. I'm just engaged to be *engaged.*

VITO. I don' understand.

IRIS. No matter. *He* does.

VITO. So. The book. Yes? You and me. *Please?*

IRIS. (*Retrieving her hand.*) Maestro, you are dripping with charm. But, for God's sake, don't drip it all over me. Because if you do, I'll succumb and it'll only be a question of time until we're both sorry.

VITO. You hear bad things of me, no?

IRIS. Yes.

VITO. From Bobby the bastard?

IRIS. And the two other bastards.

VITO. And one bitch?

IRIS. Two.

VITO. You believe?

IRIS. I'd be foolish to disbelieve *all* of them.

VITO. True. You know how is it—some peoples they bring out the worst in other peoples.

IRIS. Yes.

VITO. And some the best? Bring out?

IRIS. Of course.

VITO. Is my business. I must try always bring out the best in the soloists. Is like marriage—I know you against—but conductor and soloist—a marriage. Sometimes good. Sometimes no good. These five bitches and bastards, they bring out my worst. You can my best bring out.

IRIS. (*Finishes her drink in a gulp, gets up and prepares to leave again.*) I'm very sorry.

VITO. Maestro.

IRIS. Maestro. But I can't. And I *won't*, because—

VITO. (*Prompting.*) Because—?

IRIS. Something. Instinct. Something in the air. I just feel it would be—

VITO. Ah hah! (*HE strikes his forehead with the heel of his hand.*) I know! I see!

IRIS. What?

VITO. You afraid because you think I want to make *fohking* with you!

IRIS. Well, don't you?

VITO. (*All innocence.*) *Me?* You got these loco ideas—maleses running, fohking, fohking everybody every place. (*He laughs an unconvincing laugh.*)

IRIS. They do.

VITO. Not me. No more. I don' do no running. With you and me—how you say? Sticky business.

IRIS. Strictly.

VITO. All right.

IRIS. Actually, it was your wife's idea, too.

VITO. Sure, she's plenty brain.

IRIS. Well, give me a few days and—

VITO. Yes, you sleep with it.

IRIS. *On* it.

VITO. Wait! You going to correct me all the time I make some small mistake—

IRIS. Why not? How else are you going to learn?

VITO. *(In a temper.)* Me. I don' *got* to learn. I *know!*

IRIS. There we are. You see how impossible it would be.

VITO. No no. I want you fix my *book*. No fix me. I don' care of my English. I speak ten languages. Francais, Deutsch, Ivrit, Svenska, Espagnol, Ruski, English, Nihongo, Polska—all lousy. Even my Italian no good. *My* language—she is *music! Music!* This one I speak beautyful. Better as any*body*.

IRIS. *(Touched.)* Maestro—I'll never correct you again.

VITO. You come to Carnegie Saturday? Eight P.M.? I have The Cleveland. You have hear me conduct the Beethoven Five?

IRIS. No.

VITO. Then you have never hear it.

(HE takes the fountain pen out of her hand, turns away slightly, and using the pen as a baton, prepares to conduct. Suddenly, HE gives the downbeat, singing the opening bar of Beethoven's Fifth Symphony.

The LIGHTS dim swiftly.

As the scene darkens. The Cleveland Symphony Orchestra takes up the MUSIC and plays the next twelve bars, fading as the LIGHTS come up on Scene 3.)

ACT I

Scene 3

The LIGHTS come up to reveal that we are in one of the most attractive and charming rooms in the house, the dining room, situated on the ground floor and overlooking a lush, verdant backyard. Rachel's flower garden is varied and abundant. She cares for it herself daily, in the appropriate seasons.
The lower part of the elm can now be seen.
From upstairs, the BEETHOVEN continues softly.
The dining room furniture was designed and built and given to The Maestro by his old friend and admirer, Frank Lloyd Wright. It combines beauty and comfort and practicability. Each chair is an armchair. The table is octagonal. When there are eight at the table, each one has a different service of matching napery, silver, and china.
The cabinets and shelving suggest forever.
The paintings have been acquired across the years, not from celebrated artists or grand galleries but from student shows and flea markets and street sales. They all celebrate the glory of food and wine: a colorful French charcuterie; a glistening lobster; a tray of cheese, each with a tiny flag designating the country of its origin; a loaf of bread; three wine bottles: a red, a white, a rosé; a flowing cornucopia of fruit; a cornfield. No one has ever entered this room without his appetite being stimulated.
A decorative Japanese screen shields the swinging door to the pantry and kitchen beyond.
It is 1:10 P.M. of a sweet, sunny August day.

VITO and RACHEL are at the table. THEY are having jellied madrilène with red caviar and a sour cream topping. There is a third setting.
BRUCE and ERIC, in powder blue jackets, are serving. Eric, biscuits; Bruce, wine.
VITO, a gourmet/gourmand, is tasting and considering judiciously. RACHEL watches him. HE is about to say something. ERIC and BRUCE, too, wait for the reaction, but nothing comes. Instead, VITO takes another spoonful and tastes it as though sampling vintage wine.

VITO. (*Finally.*) Good.
RACHEL. Thank you.

(*SHE, BRUCE, and ERIC are relieved.*)

VITO. But not so good as last time.

(*RACHEL laughs musically and merrily. SHE exchanges a look with the SERVANTS who leave. VITO frowns.*)

VITO. Is funny?
RACHEL. Hilarious.
VITO. Why?
RACHEL. Because we've had this lovely jellied madrilène with red caviar and sour cream once a week in the summer months—ever since Nela Rubinstein gave you the recipe.
VITO. So?
RACHEL. And every time we have it—that's what you say.
VITO. Say what?
RACHEL. (*Imitating him remarkably.*) "Good. But not so good as a *last* time!"

VITO. You should try get rid your Italian accent.

(*THEY share a little laugh.*)

VITO. You know who had the Italian accent more bad as me? Toscanini. Because he has hated the English language. Me, I love it. I don' speak it but I love it.
RACHEL. (*Reaches over and touches his hand affectionately.*) You speak it very well—
VITO. (*Over-enunciating, especially the 'th' sound.*) Thank—you—ay—*th*ousand—*th*imes.
RACHEL. —for a foreigner.
VITO. What you mean "foreigner?"
RACHEL. You're *not?*
VITO. Maybe here I am foreigner. In Italy I am not.
RACHEL. Well, *that's* true!
VITO. In Italy *you* are foreigner!
RACHEL. No argument there.
VITO. (*Pointing his bouillon spoon at her.*) Too many times you—

(*HE stops as IRIS comes in. RACHEL rings a bell to summon Eric and Bruce.*)

IRIS. Sorry.

(*SHE goes to her place at the table. She is wearing a billowy, flowered summer frock. VITO gets up.*)

IRIS. Oh, *please* don't get up.
VITO. I *am* up.

(*HE holds her chair for her. As THEY stand next to each other, we note that they are now the same height. Of course. SHE is now wearing the flattest possible sandals—and no eyeglasses. She has acquired contact lenses.)*

IRIS. Thank you, Maestro.

(HE seats her and returns to his chair as ERIC comes in and serves Iris. BRUCE follows with wine.)

IRIS. Thank you.

(ERIC goes.)

    IRIS. I'm terribly sorry to be late.
    VITO. Me. I am *never* late.

(IRIS looks at him with meaning.)

    VITO. Only with delivering manuscripts.

(ALL THREE laugh tentatively.)

    IRIS. Not my fault really, it's just—gosh, this is delicious!
    RACHEL. You should have been here *last* time!

(VITO laughs. BRUCE leaves.)

    IRIS. It was a San Francisco call. That *beau* of mine! He's brainy as can be, but he never has been able to understand the time difference. He can't remember if it's three hours earlier here or later or four hours or what.
    VITO. Is three hours sooner there except daylight time. Then four hours.
    IRIS. Yes, I know. But *he* doesn't.

VITO. (*Showing off.*) In London is five hours *more*. In Paris six. Madrid five. Milano six. Athens seven.

(*IRIS is visibly impressed.*)

VITO. Moscow eight.
IRIS. (*Gushing.*) My!
VITO. In Tokyo is three hours more yesterday. Is simple.
IRIS. Not to my beau it's not.
VITO. (*To Rachel.*) Beau. Cosa vuol dire? Beau?
RACHEL. Vuol dire fidanzato ... Boyfriend.
VITO. (*Manages to contain his annoyance.*) What is he? This boo?
RACHEL. Beau.
VITO. Bow.
RACHEL. (*Giving up.*) Right!

(*ERIC and BRUCE come in. Throughout the following ERIC will clear skillfully and gracefully, while BRUCE offers a splendidly garnished lobster salad from a large silver platter.*)

IRIS. (*Replying to Vito.*) He's a documentary film maker.
VITO. (*To Rachel.*) Cosa diavolo è?

(*BRUCE offers the platter to Rachel.*)

RACHEL. Fa documentari come Isaac Stern che ci è piaciuto tanto. *From Mao to Mozart.*
VITO. (*To Iris.*) He make with Isaac Stern?
IRIS. Oh, no. Not that one.

(*BRUCE offers the platter to Iris.*)

VITO. (*To Rachel.*) Ma ha detto—
RACHEL. I said he makes films *like* that.
VITO. (*Understanding.*) Oh. Not music ones.

(*ERIC leaves. BRUCE offers the platter to Vito.*)

IRIS. Well, he did do one two years ago. *Wonderful.*

(*VITO is serving himself.*)

IRIS. On Zubin Mehta.

(*VITO reacts physically, and so violently that the tray and the lobster salad go all over the table, to say nothing of all over him.*
Swift, complex action: RACHEL rings the bell. ERIC comes running in and assists. BRUCE puts down the serving platter and does what he can do with the table. RACHEL works on Vito. ERIC does the floor. A new placement and napkin are provided. It is all done at high speed and in a way that makes us suspect that it has happened before.
All clear. ERIC and BRUCE leave.)

VITO. (*Quietly and calmly.*) Zubin Mehta?
IRIS. It was tremendous.
VITO. Zubin Mehta is tremendous?
IRIS. I mean the *film* was extraordinary.
VITO. Zubin Mehta is a boy. Maybe some day he can be good—like his father. Why he choosed him? Your bough.
RACHEL. Boo.
VITO. Beau.

(*RACHEL nods, pleased with herself.*)

IRIS. Well, *he* didn't choose him. The Philharmonic did and then they asked Larry to do it.
VITO. Larry.
IRIS. It was only a little short. Two reels.
VITO. Oh? Only two?
IRIS. —ran about fifteen minutes.
VITO. Is *enough*, is enough.

(*ALL THREE are eating now.*)

VITO. How long this buoy—is your friendly boy?
IRIS. About three years. And he's not a buoy, exactly. He's thirty-four.
VITO. You make fun my English speaking?
IRIS. I?
RACHEL. Oh, don't pay any attention to him, dear. He's miffed because I twitted him about his accent.
VITO. I *like* my accent! Is *charming*. (*To Iris.*) No?
IRIS. You *really* want to know what I think?
VITO. *Yes!*
IRIS. I think your accent is charming.
VITO. You understand what I say? Always?
IRIS. Of course.
VITO. (*To Rachel.*) Ecco! I tell her my Kiepura story. Funny. Yes?
RACHEL. Now?
VITO. Yes, *now!*
RACHEL. Very well. (*SHE sighs.*)
VITO. I know you hear it before but—
RACHEL. *Many* times.
VITO. How many?
RACHEL. Seven hundred?
VITO. But this time maybe for the book.

IRIS. (*Getting out her steno pad.*) Let's hear it. (*To Rachel.*) We're short on light stuff.

RACHEL. All right. But I think we should separate work from lunch.

IRIS. You're quite right, Mrs. De Angelis. Sorry.

(*SHE puts away her steno pad as ERIC comes in.*)

VITO. (*Trying again.*) Jan Kiepura—

ERIC. Excuse me. Telephone, Miss Peabody. Little, Brown, Boston. I told them you were at lunch, but they said it was urgent.

IRIS. Urgent?

RACHEL. Oh, go on.

IRIS. Excuse me, please.

(*SHE hurries out. ERIC goes.*)

VITO. Too nervous girl.

RACHEL. Well, it's a nervous time. Deadlines are always maddening. Can you imagine people saying to Bach, "Hurry up! Hurry up! We need that cantata by Wednesday night!"

VITO. That's what they always *do* say to Bach.

RACHEL. Really?

VITO. Why you think he writes so many? Had to. Mozart, too.

RACHEL. Well, as I always say, deadlines are marvelous. They make you get things done.

VITO. You know why we got The Goldberg Variations? Because—because Count Keyserling suffered from insomnia—

VITO/RACHEL. (*In unison.*) —and hired Bach to write some music for his pianist Goldberg to play to put him to sleep.

VITO. (*A pause.*) Why she so nervous, this nervous girl?

RACHEL. I think *you* **make** her nervous.

VITO. I think *you* make her.

RACHEL. How?

VITO. Don' don' don'. Too much don'. She want to make the notes—you say don' don' don'.

RACHEL. Perhaps you're right.

VITO. You think so?

RACHEL. Yes. This is a different sort of time. The project. An emergency, in a way. (*SHE touches him.*) You won't hear another don't don't don't out of me. Whatever's best for the book is what we'll do.

VITO. (*Tenderly.*) You are very nice.

RACHEL. So are you.

VITO. Thank you.

RACHEL. (*To herself.*) Sometimes.

VITO. (*Having heard it.*) Shaddop!

(*THEY eat and think for a moment. VITO gets up and paces about.*)

VITO. (*Carefully.*) Cara mia—when you say what is best for book we do—you mean it?

RACHEL. I think I do. Why?

VITO. Because—about the tour—

RACHEL. (*Apprehensively.*) Yes ...?

VITO. Will be most very hard this time. The travel, the rehearse, the performance—

RACHEL. And?

VITO. Interview interview interview. (*RACHEL waits.*) Meetings. You know.

RACHEL. So ...?

VITO. *And* the *book!* Madonna mia, The Book!

RACHEL. Yes.

VITO. I wish I never sign that contract. You told me yes, remember?

RACHEL. We needed the money. Remember?

VITO. But I don' like this talking of myself all the day. I don' like to know myself too good. Many things I don' want to remember.

RACHEL. I know.

VITO. So me, I talk talk talk. She, this one, asks to me questions— too many questions. When I don' answer she get mad. Yesterday she begin asking too much about our son. Why Antonio do the crazy terrible thing he do to himself.

(RACHEL is all at once pained; VITO, on the verge of tears.)

RACHEL. Don't, Vito!

VITO. I tell her, I don' know. I will *never* know.

RACHEL. I'll speak to her.

IRIS. *(Bounces back in, beaming.)* They *love* the new chunk.

VITO. Chunk?

IRIS. Of the book. They *love* it! Yay! *(SHE twirls about happily.)*

VITO. *(Goes behind the screen and calls.)* Eric! Bring now one Dom Perignon.

RACHEL. What fine news!

IRIS. *(Sits down and stretches out in her chair.)* Whew!

VITO. I not surprised. I know it was great.

IRIS. Of course now they're pressing even harder for time. I said, "God, Roger! You're like that Hollywood producer screaming, 'I don't want it *good*, I want it *Tuesday*.'"

(*ERIC comes in bearing a tray on which there is an ice bucket holding a bottle of Dom Perignon and three Baccarat flute glasses. HE sets it down and begins to remove the foil.*)

VITO. No, no. (*HE takes over.*) You bring two more glass.
ERIC. Certainly, Maestro.
VITO. And Eric.
ERIC. Bruce.
VITO. Bruce.

(*ERIC goes.*)

VITO. Irish, you like it, champagne?
IRIS. Love it.
VITO. Me, I hate it. Champagne, even pink, I hate. But Dom Perignon, I love it. (*He opens the bottle of Dom Perignon. HE does so with extraordinary style and grace and expertise. He is showing off, of course. No posh sommelier could outdo his performance.*) You know why? Because was important part of my first love-doing. When I was thirteen – fourteen. I drank it one whole bottle of Dom Perignon and became the man.

(*The cork pops. ERIC and BRUCE come in. VITO pours.*)

VITO. Rachel. (*He pours.*) Irish. (*Pours. To Bruce.*) Eric.
BRUCE. Bruce.
VITO. (*To Eric.*) Bruce.
ERIC. Eric.
VITO. To MAESTRO—by Vito De Angelis!
RACHEL. (*To herself.*) More or less.

(*Glasses are clinked and ALL drink.*)

VITO. (*To Eric and Bruce sounding a bit like Iris.*) They love the new chink of the book!
BRUCE. I'm *thrilled*—
ERIC. —Maestro.

(*ALL drink again. Then ERIC and BRUCE discreetly disappear. VITO, RACHEL, and IRIS resume their lunch.*)

VITO. (*Looking toward the kitchen.*) Fine boys. Mans. Like family. They do everything—the cook—the clean—
RACHEL. They do windows.
VITO. Massage sometimes. (*He motions to Iris and leans forward toward her.*) They are *pan – sees*.
IRIS. (*Taken aback.*) How can you be sure?
VITO. (*Logically.*) They love the ballet.
RACHEL. And what's more—

(*ERIC and BRUCE come in. During the following, THEY clear, and serve a lemon soufflé.*)

RACHEL. Iris, dear, change of mind, change of plan. Do get your notebook out. We *will* work during meals.

(*IRIS swiftly gets out her notebook.*)

RACHEL. Next time I'll remember to bring my Flents.

(*IRIS look confused.*)

VITO. (*Explains with appropriate gestures.*) Ear stop-ups.
BRUCE. (*Just before leaving.*) The bubbly—

ERIC. —was delicious.
BRUCE. Maestro.

(*BRUCE and ERIC leave.*)

VITO. What means bubbling?
RACHEL. The champagne.
VITO. Was Dom Perignon.
IRIS. I think—
RACHEL. Let it go, dear. Let it go.
VITO. (*After a deep breath.*) Jan Kiepura. You know who is he? *Was* he? Now dead?
IRIS. No.
VITO. (*Automatically.*) Maestro.
IRIS. Maestro.
VITO. Was big beautyful Polish tenor. Very good in operetta. *The Merry Widow.* (*HE sings and conducts a few bars.*) Offenbach. (*HE sings and conducts a few bars from Tales of Hoffman.*) *Rosenkavalier.* (*HE sings and conducts a few bars of Rosenkavalier waltz.*) He is married —was— with soprano—Marta Eggerth. Also good. So. In New York they do *Waltzertraum*. Strauss. Oscar Strauss. Beautyful. In English. (*HE sings and conducts with his fork.*) I am young – not yet great – I need job – I am conducting. Comes dress rehearsal for Shuberts. Finish first act. Trouble. Mr. Lee Shubert comes down to pit and he say to Kiepura—no, not say, say loud, holler, "God damn it, Kiepura, I don' understand one single word you say or sing." Was true. Kiepura say, "Yes, I know, Mr. Shubert, but not worry. Before opening night I will pohlish opp my English." And I say—me—I say, "Maybe better, Kiepura, you English opp your Pohlish!"

(*IRIS laughs, too hard. RACHEL closes her eyes in relief.*)

IRIS. (*Writing.*) Oh, that's priceless, Maestro! *Priceless!* "Maybe better if—"

VITO. No, no! *No* "if"—

VITO/IRIS. (*Together.*) "Maybe better you English up your Pohlish!"

VITO. (*Laughs.*) Was good, heh? "Maybe better you English opp your Pohlish."

RACHEL. Oh, my God! (*To Iris.*) I'll be fascinated to see how you use that. Awkward to have him repeat his own joke.

IRIS. (*Thinking hard.*) Maybe we could have the Maestro *tell* it—but then give the punchline to Mr. Lee Shubert.

RACHEL. Say, you're clever.

VITO. What is it? What?

RACHEL. Puoi dirlo nel libro, ma è Mr. *Shubert* che dice: "Maybe better you English up your Polish."

(*VITO stands. All at once HE seems to be six-four. HE glares at Iris.*)

VITO. (*Too softly.*) *My* joke for *Shubert?*

IRIS. Just an idea.

VITO. (*His voice rising to fortissimo.*) One more idea like so and I *throw you out!!* (*HE storms out of the room.*)

IRIS. (*Defeated.*) I think I'd better quit.

RACHEL. He'll be contrite in twenty minutes.

IRIS. I've got to be more careful.

RACHEL. Not necessarily. When he yells, yell back.

IRIS. Oh, Lord, I haven't the strength. When Larry and I get into one of our screamers, I have to go to bed for a day to recover. I'm afraid I—

VITO. (*Returns. HE is thinking. Suddenly.*) You know what would be good?

IRIS. What?

VITO. If Mr. Lee *Shubert* would say, "Maybe you should English opp your Pohlish!"

(*HE smiles beatifically as IRIS and RACHEL exchange a woman-to-woman look. VITO refills the three glasses and offers a toast.*)

VITO. To the tour.
IRIS. The tour.
RACHEL. The tour.

(*THEY drink. VITO sits. ERIC and BRUCE come in and clear and leave.*)

IRIS. Exactly how long *is* the tour, Maestro?
VITO. Six weeks only.
RACHEL. We've often done twenty to thirty weeks at a stretch.
VITO. (*Reflectively.*) To me, the most important thing in life is to keep my baton busy!
RACHEL. (*Almost to herself.*) And you certainly *try!*
IRIS. Maestro, do you ever find—?
ERIC. (*Comes in.*) Sorry, Miss Peabody. Telephone.
IRIS. Say I'll call back.
ERIC. (*With meaning.*) It's San Francisco.
IRIS. Oh. (*To Vito and Rachel.*) Forgive me, please. (*SHE is flustered but on her way out.*) It must be something awfully— (*SHE is gone.*)
VITO. (*Irritated.*) Next book I hire a eunuch.

(*ERIC leaves, not without registering this last remark.*)

RACHEL. Do you remember that glorious idea I once had?
VITO. Which one?

RACHEL. To get rid of every telephone in the house—except one to call out on in case of emergency?
VITO. We *do* it!
RACHEL. You'd last a week, if that.
VITO. Peoples would think I crazy.

(*RACHEL smiles.*)

VITO. I know. They think so any*how*.
RACHEL. (*Looking at him long and hard.*) I really love you, my dear man. More than ever.
VITO. (*Comes to her.*) And I you.

(*THEY embrace and kiss in a special way.*)

RACHEL. You were saying?
VITO. About what?
RACHEL. About me not coming on the tour with you this time.
VITO. I say that?
RACHEL. No, but you were *going* to.
VITO. How you think you know?
RACHEL. Dear heart. There are many disadvantages in a long, long marriage. I've heard all your jokes. I know all your symptoms. And there are so few surprises. But there are advantages, too. After thirty years I know exactly what you're thinking and feeling—no matter what you're doing or saying. We live together inside the same head.
VITO. I was thinking what it would be the best for *you*.
RACHEL. And the book?
VITO. Yes, maybe poco poco the book.
RACHEL. And Iris? A few floating fantasies there, perhaps?
VITO. No no no!

RACHEL. No?
VITO. No. She has the beau.
RACHEL. Boo.
VITO. She is too young.
RACHEL. Yes, but you're not too old ... Tell the truth—some little twitch of maybe maybe —if if —?
VITO. (*Laughing.*) Oh, Rachel, Rachel! You know me too good. (*HE comes to her.*) You come on the tour. Sure.
RACHEL. No.
VITO. (*Astounded.*)No!?
RACHEL. No. Perhaps it's time for a little break. Let what happens happen. I wouldn't want you to feel that it wasn't happening because I was there. In the way, you might say. No. You go off and do your stuff and have your triumph and write your book and whatever whatever and then, when you come back—
IRIS. (*Returns.*) He won't call here again. I promise. I made *him* promise. (*SHE sits and has her coffee.*)
RACHEL. Oh, that must be cold—let me get you some hot—
IRIS. No. No, really. I *like* warm coffee.
VITO. (*Brightly.*) *I* like warm coffee *too!*
RACHEL. (*To herself.*) Oh, brother!
IRIS. It was just that Larry has this wild idea. He thinks he could make a terrific little film of the tour.
VITO. Which tour?
IRIS. *Your* tour.

(*VITO is about to explode. RACHEL is trying to contain laughter.*)

IRIS. You know, follow you around with a hand-held Eyemo—
VITO. Eyemo?

IRIS. Camera—or maybe videotape—the travel, rehearsals, backstage stuff. But of course he has to find someone to put up the money.

RACHEL. *I'll* put up the money!

VITO. How much cost a thing like this?

IRIS. Not much. Two or three hundred thousand.

VITO. Would be eccellente! (*VITO is upset. Too many conflicting emotions are crossing through his psyche at one and the same time. His yen for Iris. Rachel being on to him. And now this—yes, a film would be fine. But does it have to be this beau bastard making it?*) Scusi. I go to pee. (*HE wanders out.*)

RACHEL. Iris, dear. Vito asked me to speak to you about—

IRIS. Yes?

RACHEL. Can't certain matters, personal ones—too personal—simply be omitted or glossed over?

IRIS. I think you and The Maestro can trust my taste—judgment—as to what goes in or stays out. And in any case the final say is yours.

(*VITO wanders back in, goes to the champagne bottle, finds a few drops, pours them into his glass and drinks.*)

RACHEL. Let's do it this way. If you ask him something that he's reluctant to discuss—ask *me* and *I'll* tell you.

VITO. *You* tell?

RACHEL. Yes, *I* tell. I thought you—

VITO. (*At the top of his lungs.*) Is *my* book! *My* life! *I* tell—not you.

RACHEL. (*Placating him.*) All right, darling. All right.

VITO. (*Still up there.*) You want tell? Write your own book—not write mine! Write your *own* book.

RACHEL. Maybe I *will!*

(*There is an awkward pause.*)

IRIS. If you do, Rachel—will you let me see it first?
VITO. Shaddop!
IRIS. (*Topping him.*) *Shaddop yourself!!*

(*A tense, anything-can-happen pause. Then:*)

VITO. (*Suddenly deflated.*) Sure, sure. (*To Iris, with his most winning smile.*) Why you so excitement?
IRIS. I'm not excitement.
RACHEL. We'll see, honey. We'll see. (*The LIGHTS fade.*)

CURTAIN

ACT II

Scene 1

We are back in the study where we began. Almost two months have passed, and the new season is reflected in a change of flowers. The bright vivid summer spectrum has been replaced by gentle autumnal hues.

It is a late afternoon in October and we are aware of the fact that no music is playing.

However, from the corner of Forty-seventh Street and Second Avenue, the spirited sound of Trinidadian STEEL PANS are heard.

RACHEL, wearing a colorful Chanel tweed suit, is dictating to ROBERT. SHE moves about the room—sitting, standing, sprawling, as she digs into herself for the right word, or idea or expression, or memory.

Robert's jacket hangs on the back of his chair; he wears a vest and his tie is loosened.

RACHEL. —but with Vito and me—it was a case of "*loathe* at first sight."

(*ROBERT laughs lightly.*)

RACHEL. You don't think that's just a bit tacky, that joke?
ROBERT. Not at all. So. (*HE reads.*) "—but with Vito and me it was a case of *loathe* at first sight."
RACHEL. (*Dictating again.*) At that time, my Italian was sketchy and his English was non-existent. So communication was— (*SHE stops talking and moving.*

SHE thinks hard, then looks up at the ceiling for a moment. Finishing her sentence.) —perplexing.

ROBERT. Good.

RACHEL. *(Goes to the bar tray and pours herself a glass of Mountain Valley water.)* Have you ever noticed— *(SHE holds up the bottle.)* Want some?

ROBERT. No, thanks.

RACHEL. —how often the word you're looking for is on the ceiling?

ROBERT. *(Smiles. Reading from his notes.)* "So communication was perplexing."

RACHEL. *(Thinks for a beat before continuing.)* It must be noted that although the war had been over for some time, the embers of enmity were still smoldering fiercely beneath the polite surface.

ROBERT. Beautiful!

RACHEL. Are you flattering me for some reason, Bobby? Or just because you're a dear fellow?

ROBERT. I'm flattering you not at all.

RACHEL. Oh, hell!

ROBERT. Why?

RACHEL. Because if there's one thing in life I *adore*, it's flattery.

ROBERT. *(Laughing.)* I'll do my best.

RACHEL. Oh—speaking of flattery—did I tell you Irving hates the title?

ROBERT. MRS. MAESTRO? He hates that?

RACHEL. Yes.

ROBERT. Well, he's wrong. I know he's a powerhouse agent but that doesn't make him an expert on titles.

RACHEL. Maybe it's because he represents Vito and *his* book, too.

ROBERT. Doubtless. By the way, does Vito know he's representing *you*?

RACHEL. He doesn't even know I'm writing a book.

ROBERT. (*Amazed.*) What?

RACHEL. He'll find out soon enough. (*SHE looks at her watch.*) Any minute now. They should've been here an hour ago. Plane late, probably.

ROBERT. (*Putting on his jacket.*) I'm leaving.

RACHEL. Why, for heaven's sake?

ROBERT. I took it for granted—I don't know why—that he *knew* about this project. I certainly don't want to be in the room—or in the house, even, when he finds out. Or in New York City. Or New York *State!*

RACHEL. But why should he object? He suggested it.

ROBERT. He did?

RACHEL. Of course. He said, "Write your own book." In fact, he said it twice.

ROBERT. And did he also suggest that you do it with me?

RACHEL. (*Thinks.*) I don't think so.

ROBERT. And how's he going to react to *that* idea?

RACHEL. Apoplectically, I hope.

ROBERT. Goodbye.

RACHEL. Don't be silly.

ROBERT. Silly? Do you remember my last encounter with him in this room? It was like being in an earthquake—one that was out to get me personally. No, no. Let me go—I'll move back in after you tell him: (a) that you're writing a book; (b) that Irving's your agent; and (c) God help us all—that you're doing it with *me*. Until then—

VITO'S VOICE. (*Booms out in the hall.*) Hollo!

RACHEL. Too late.

ROBERT. Damn!

VITO'S VOICE. Hollo!

RACHEL. Hollo!

VITO'S VOICE. We home! (*VITO comes into the study. HE stands for a moment arms outstretched.*)

VITO. Bon voyage!

(*HE has not yet removed his fur-collared coat, nor his large cashmere hat from Gelot, Paris, nor his beige kid gloves. HE goes at once to Rachel, embraces her, kisses her again and again and begins to cry. SHE comforts him. HE is facing away from ROBERT who takes this opportunity to get out. As HE nears the door, however, IRIS comes in. She has taken off her hat and coat. SHE almost collides with Robert.*)

IRIS. Bob!

(*THEY embrace and kiss each other's cheeks. They are old pals. On the word "Bob," VITO stops crying and gives a start in the manner of a man who has been stabbed in the back. HE turns—in slow motion— in time to see the kissing. VITO and ROBERT exchange a long look. VITO and RACHEL exchange a longer look. VITO and IRIS exchange the longest look. Then IRIS-RACHEL; ROBERT-IRIS; ROBERT-RACHEL.*
We note that VITO is now a shade taller than Iris. SHE is still in flats, HE has taken to wearing lifts.
VITO starts moving toward Robert. ROBERT stands his ground.)

VITO. (*In all cordiality.*) Bob! (*HE embraces him.*) What you are doing here? I thought you go back to Nova Scotia.
ROBERT. Martha's Vineyard.

(*ERIC and BRUCE come in with the tea tables. THEY wear pastel green jackets. VITO goes to them and embraces each one in turn.*)

VITO. *(To Bruce.)* Eric! Bon voyage!
BRUCE. Bruce.
VITO. *(To Eric.)* Bruce! Bon voyage!
ERIC. Eric.
VITO. Welcome home!
ERIC. Thank you.
BRUCE. Maestro.

(HE takes Vito's hat and coat. RACHEL begins serving tea.)

RACHEL. *(To Robert.)* He gets them right sometimes.

(ERIC and BRUCE leave.)

VITO. *(To Robert.)* So you know Miss Pea*body*, no?
ROBERT. Yes.
IRIS. Yes. Bobby's done seven books for me.
ROBERT. Seven and a half, actually.
VITO. A half?

(An awkward pause. A touchy subject.)

RACHEL. Tea, everyone!
ROBERT. I really must go.
RACHEL. Go where? You *live* here.

(VITO's teacup breaks the law of gravity and goes flying off in the manner of the lobster in Act I. This time it is worse. The tea is hot. VITO is scalded, screams, jumps up and upsets one of the tea tables. ERIC and BRUCE run in. The room is suddenly a mess. Moreover, this time there are more helping hands, adding to the confusion. ERIC and BRUCE, ROBERT and IRIS and RACHEL all work away until everything is put right.

ERIC and BRUCE leave. The OTHERS resume the places and attitudes they had before the accident. RACHEL pours expertly and graciously throughout the following.)

RACHEL. Cream or lemon?
IRIS. Both. No. Neither.
VITO. Houston was great. Fifteen calls.
IRIS. Sixteen, Maestro.
VITO. I think only fifteen.
IRIS. And San Francisco—eighteen.
VITO. San Francisco they always applaud much.
RACHEL. The cold and damp I expect.

(ROBERT laughs and makes a note.)

VITO. In Los Angeles I broke one flute player. Missed two cues in the Brahms. *(HE does the flute.)* Eeedle eedle eedle eedle pahh! I kicked him.
RACHEL. —kicked him *out?*
IRIS. No, *kicked* him.
VITO. Was a great tour.*(And now MAESTRO VITO DE ANGELIS—or more specifically, the actor playing him—performs an astonishing tour de force. HE takes us on the six week tour, conducting eight different orchestras and six soloists. We will hear string sections, solo flutes, percussion, brass sections, violin solos, piano solos, full orchestral swells, everything.)* In Detroit, we do Mahler ... *(Performing the Mahler Ninth, in full voice, HE reproduces the climax with the Chorale.)* Chicago, all Tchaikovsky— fiddle concerto with Itzhak—easy. We do it many times. *(HE renders the key theme of Tchaikovsky's Violin Concerto in D, movingly. We should be able to hear the passionate, sighing violin.)*

RACHEL. (*All maternal sympathy.*) What's a matter, Tchaikovsky?

VITO. Cleveland. One Mozart. (*He whips through the opening of the Concerto in A for Clarinet.*) One Brahms. (*HE draws the lush sounds of Brahms Symphony Number Three in F from his unseen orchestra.*) One Ravel. (*With overwhelming tenderness he suffers through part of Pavanne For a Dead Princess.*) Houston. Two Beethoven. The Five and the Seven. (*HE somehow manages to perform and conduct Beethoven's Fifth and Seventh Symphonies simultaneously.*) One Haydn. (*HE becomes an orchestra playing Haydn's Concerto in E-Flat For Trumpet and Orchestra.*) San Francisco. Chopin with Weissenberg piano. (*HE performs Concerto Number Two in F For Piano.*) Los Angeles. Prokofiev. (*A snatch from Peter and the Wolf.*) Shostakovich. (*The opening of Shostakovich's Fourth Symphony.*) Victor Herbert. (*HE blasts out the finish of Babes in Toyland.*) That's all.

IRIS. I'm exhausted.

RACHEL. And how's the book coming?

(*VITO and IRIS exchange a look.*)

IRIS. Well, to tell the truth—

RACHEL. Oh, *do!*

IRIS. —not well.

VITO. No time. No time. People—stupid people think conductor stands up, throws the arms—is his job. Is the nothing of his job. Preparation. Preparation. Takes the time.

RACHEL. (*To Iris.*) You should've come home when you saw it wasn't going to—

IRIS. The Maestro kept thinking things would—

VITO. Yes, yes. Well—(*HE is anxious to change the subject.*) And what you doing now, Bob?

(*ROBERT stalls by gulping some tea.*)

RACHEL. He's helping me to write *my* book: MRS. MAESTRO.

(*There is no stopping it. VITO is propelled to his feet like Hugo Zachinni, the human cannonball. HIS cup and saucer make a second journey. ERIC and BRUCE arrive with dispatch. ERIC manages, miraculously, to catch the cup; BRUCE gets the saucer.*)

ERIC. Jesus—
BRUCE. Christ!

(*The clean-up TEAM goes to work. It takes less time this time. After all, they are becoming practiced. In a thrice, all is as before. ERIC and BRUCE leave. There is a moment of polite tea drinking.*)

VITO. (*Finally, to Rachel.*) Is that so?
ROBERT. (*To Iris.*) She's a real writer, Bunny. Keep an eye on her.
VITO. Who is Bunny?
IRIS. Oh—just a silly nickname.
VITO. I don' like it. (*To Rachel.*) You are calling your book the name MRS. MAESTRO?
RACHEL. Nice, isn't it?
VITO. *Change* it!
RACHEL. Why?
VITO. I don' like it.
RACHEL. Neither does my agent. Irving Paul Lazar.

(*This announcement sends VITO flying up again, but this time THEY are ready for him. RACHEL grabs his cup.*

ROBERT steadies one tea table while IRIS guards the other. Disaster is avoided.)

RACHEL. Do you mind us having the same agent?
VITO. He is not my agent.
RACHEL. I thought he was.
VITO. No more. Not since now. Call him up Irish and tell him he is finish.
IRIS. I'm afraid that's impossible, Maestro. He has your contract.
VITO. I can't fire him?
IRIS. No.
VITO. Then I kill him.
RACHEL. *Not* a good idea.
VITO. When you book will be finish?
RACHEL. When will *yours?*
VITO. *(To Iris.)* When?
IRIS. That depends on you, Maestro.
VITO. Quick. No more tour now. We finish quick.
IRIS. Good.
VITO. Maybe two weeks.
IRIS. Oh, I doubt that.
VITO. Maybe three weeks.
IRIS. Make it six.
RACHEL. Bobby?
ROBERT. About four weeks.
VITO. *(To Iris.)* Three weeks.
RACHEL. Sort of like Sotheby's, isn't it?

(SHE and ROBERT laugh. Vito and Iris do not. Another polite tea drinking pause.)

IRIS. Houston was beautiful.
ROBERT. *(A pause.)* Is this Earl Grey tea?
RACHEL. No. Hu-Kwa.

ROBERT. Delicious.
VITO. Is cat piss! (*HE goes to the bar tray and takes a swig of vodka. The longest pause of them all. Bottle in hand.*) Cara mia—I may see you for one two minutes?
RACHEL. Of course.
IRIS. (*Rising.*) Why don't we go.
ROBERT. Yes.
VITO. *NO!*

(*ROBERT and IRIS sit.*)

RACHEL. Excuse us, please?
VITO. (*Beaming.*) Don't go. We be right back. In sixteen bars.
RACHEL. (*To Robert, surreptitiously and definitely.*) *Don't go!*

(*HE signals his assent. VITO, still clutching the bottle, politely escorts RACHEL to the door, follows her and closes it.*)

IRIS. How's the Island?
ROBERT. Still there, thank God.
IRIS. Good.
ROBERT. How's Larry?
IRIS. Still there.
ROBERT. You didn't say, "thank God."
IRIS. Didn't I?

(*Now, as suddenly as a breaking thunderstorm, from above, we hear VITO's voice raised in shattering anger. HE is shouting—in Italian. To our amazement, we next hear RACHEL topping him in both emotion and volume. Remember she is a trained singer with a cultivated and powerful voice.*)

The volume of the sounds of battle fluctuate as the participants go up and down the stairs. [For text of offstage argument, see dialogue immediately following final scene.]
During the above:)

    ROBERT. What's happening at Little, Brown?
    IRIS. Oh, you know publishing. Musical chairs.

(*THEY continue their small talk and pretend to ignore the upstairs excitement where VITO, in an attempt to outshout Rachel, cracks his voice. Still HE continues. RACHEL does not wait for him to stop, but overlaps. THEY are both at the top of their lungs, 7.8 on the Richter Scale. For a time they sound like two hysterical viragos in vocal combat. Even those of us who have no Italian recognize that some extremely bad language is being exchanged.*
ERIC and BRUCE come in and clear. THEY, too, appear to be oblivious to the goings-on above.)

    ERIC. (*To Iris.*) Good trip—
    BRUCE. —Miss Peabody?
    IRIS. Fascinating.
    BRUCE. But tiring—
    ERIC. —I'll bet.
    IRIS. Indeed.
    ERIC. Have you been up—
    BRUCE. —to your room yet?
    IRIS. No.
    BRUCE. Oh—wait till you see it.
    ERIC. She's redone it.
    BRUCE. It's adorable.
    ERIC. We helped her.
    BRUCE. It's really *divine!*

IRIS. Well, thank you.
BRUCE and ERIC. (*Together.*) Not at all. (*THEY are gone.*)
ROBERT. It *is* splendid, I must say.
IRIS. You've seen it?
ROBERT. She showed it to me. It's right across from *my* room.
IRIS. Bob ...
ROBERT. Yes?
IRIS. Listen—I *know* it seems inappropriate—unseemly, even—but, Bob, this is something I've—it's like nothing I've ever even *read* about—let alone known.
ROBERT. (*Kindly.*) Hero worship, maybe, a little?
IRIS. It was at first, yes. But it's all changed now. I live in another world. He makes me into a better person ... I wake up every morning thinking of him. And every time I see him I feel—gratitude.
ROBERT. Careful, though. You're sure it's him you love and not his image?
IRIS. Now, how would I know that? I love what he is and was and is going to be. And I love *us*—the idea of *us*. And even though we've never said "I love you" to each other—well, not in those words, anyway—I know that he does and that I do. Maybe we don't say it because it's something *more* than love ...

(*The NOISE from above stops so abruptly that ROBERT and IRIS spring to their feet. What could have happened? Simultaneous coronaries? Murder? THEY look up through the ceiling and at each other. THEY communicate wordlessly. Should we do anything? The door opens. VITO and RACHEL come in, cheerfully. HE still carries the bottle—upside down.*)

RACHEL. There we are! That didn't take long, did it?

VITO. Business. (*HE goes to a wall panel and touches a button on the stereo master control. The dulcet sounds of Delius fill the room: A Walk Through Paradise Garden.*)

RACHEL. (*Sotto voce to Robert.*) His ace is trumped. I've always been President of our corporation. Ha!

VITO. (*To Iris, pointing to a speaker.*) My Delius. With The Tokyo. Superb. Delius he is much Japanese. (*HE looks about.*) What happened the tea?

RACHEL. I'll get it back. (*SHE starts out.*)

VITO. No, no.

(*SHE stops.*)

VITO. To hell with tea. Basta! We all have drink now!

RACHEL. (*Happily.*) Why not?

(*VITO starts for the bar tray. ROBERT intercepts him.*)

ROBERT. Let me.

VITO. (*Magnanimously.*) Why not?

ROBERT. (*At the bar tray.*) Martinis O.K.? I'm an expert.

IRIS. White wine for me.

ROBERT. Right. (*Fixes the drinks during the following.*)

VITO. I have a big suggest.

RACHEL. Yes, darling?

VITO. I take us everybody out for dinner

RACHEL. Lovely. I'll tell the boys to stop.

VITO. They come too if they want.

RACHEL. I'll ask them. (*SHE goes out.*)

VITO. What the hell. We been away so long—we find some place great. (*To Iris.*) *You* choose.

IRIS. Well, let's see. Barbetta's, San Domenico's, Romeo Salta's?

VITO. What you talking—? That's all Italian!
IRIS. Yes.
VITO. I *hate* Italian—I had enough Italian for two lifes!
RACHEL. (*Returns.*) They'd love to.
VITO. Where we go, cara mia?
RACHEL. Grenouille? Le Cirque? Chantilly?
VITO. (*Suddenly.*) *I got it!* We go downtown to Ratners.
RACHEL. But they don't take reservations.
VITO. To hell. I stand in the line! People stand in the line to see me! I stand in the line to see Ratners.
IRIS. That's terribly exciting news, Rachel—about your book.
RACHEL. Yes, isn't it?
IRIS. I'm dying to read it.
RACHEL. Well, you will soon enough.

(*VITO listens with interest but says nothing. The fact that he has been checkmated upstairs colors his behavior. HE floats over to the bar tray and hovers impatiently.*)

IRIS. (*To Rachel.*) I hope you won't think I'm prying—
RACHEL. I won't if you aren't.
IRIS. But—do you have a publisher?
RACHEL. Oh, I'm leaving that all to Irving.
IRIS. May I speak to him?
RACHEL. By all means.
IRIS. Because I have an idea that might just be *super!*
RACHEL. What is it?

(*The martinis are finished. While ROBERT fixes Iris's white wine, VITO takes the shaker and begins to drink out of it. It contains three martinis, remember. Maybe more.*

ROBERT brings Iris her drink. When HE returns to pour the martinis, HE cannot find the shaker. He is mystified until HE looks across the room and sees VITO drinking out of it. HE leaves and returns shortly with another shaker and makes another batch. Meanwhile:)

IRIS. Wouldn't it be stupendous—if we could buy your book from Irving and then arrange to have them published simultaneously?

RACHEL. Would it?

IRIS. Fan*ta*stic! (*SHE places posters in the air.*) MAESTRO by Vito De Angelis. MRS. MAESTRO by Rachel Garland De Angelis.

(*VITO, horrified at this idea, finishes the contents of the shaker in one long draught.*)

IRIS. (*Continuing—on fire.*) They might even have sort of matching bindings and could be marketed as a set – boxed.

RACHEL. (*With a glance in Vito's direction.*) But what about the people who are only interested in *mine?*

ROBERT. Yes.

(*VITO pours gin into the empty shaker and begins to drink again.*)

IRIS. The sets would be only for those who want both.

RACHEL. You'd better let me talk that over with Irving. And Bobby.

VITO. (*Rather pathetically.*) And me?

RACHEL. Certainly and you, my love.

(*VITO manages a pained smile.*)

IRIS. Rachel—I *do* thank you for my room. The boys told me.
RACHEL. Oh, those big-mouths. It was meant to be a *surprise*.
IRIS. I'm sure it will be.
RACHEL. I hope you won't mind about the bed.
IRIS. The bed?
RACHEL. I took out the twins and put in a king-size.
IRIS. Oh, I *love* a big bed!

(*VITO takes another gulp, empties the shaker and returns unsteadily to the tray. HE pours again but does not drink—yet.*)

RACHEL. It's almost impossible to find one in a hotel these days.
IRIS. I know. (*Is she blushing?*)
VITO. (*Waving the shaker.*) No—not alm*ost* impossible. All-impossible. (*HE looks at Iris.*) But—what the hell—we fool them, hey? We move the twins together and put the mattresses—

(*HE gestures suiting the action to the word. HE pushes two armchairs together. HE stretches across the two chairs as IRIS tries to grab him.*)

IRIS. Vito—!

(*VITO falls off the chairs, realizing his gaffe. IRIS gets her briefcase and purse and runs out of the room. VITO looks at Rachel, looks for Iris.*)

VITO. Irish? (*HE gets up and goes through the door, calling.*) Irish?

(RACHEL re-arranges the armchairs, then stands quietly for a moment. VITO, at the door, shrugs apologetically. About the accident? About the revelation? Even he doesn't know.)

ROBERT. End of chapter?
RACHEL. No. *Beginning!*

(The LIGHTS fade. The DELIUS swells and plays until the lights come up on Scene 2.)

ACT II
Scene 2

The DELIUS changes to the Rachmaninoff Third Piano Concerto as the LIGHTS come up on the sitting room.
Two months have gone by. It is a bright December morning. The sun floods in, making the entrancing room even more entrancing. A fine fire burns gently in the fireplace. RACHEL wears a long, flowing lavender housecoat. ROBERT, in loafers and slacks and sweater, sits in an armchair reading from a typescript.

ROBERT. "—and so I was nonplussed when he proposed marriage. I suspect that *he* was even *more* nonplussed. After all, I was expecting a proposition and instead received a proposal. My acceptance was delayed for well over six months because he made it a condition that I give up my career for good and all. I resisted it powerfully, but he argued that two careers in one family would be impossible. In time, I was convinced. Now, looking back, I see that it was a fatal blunder. True, being Mrs. Maestro has been a career of sorts—but one of service rather than self-expression. Following our marriage—"

(*The intercom CHIMES sound. The theme from César Franck's Symphony in D. RACHEL responds.*)

VITO'S VOICE. When the doctor comes you send him up right away quick, yes?
RACHEL. Yes.
VITO'S VOICE. Goddam it! (*He switches off.*)
ROBERT. Boy, he's a real pain in the neck today.
RACHEL. Why elevate him?
ROBERT. (*Indicates the intercom.*) Can we shut that off?
RACHEL. But then we'll have *him* down here.
ROBERT. Right. (*HE resumes the reading.*) "Following our marriage we formulated a plan of life and agreed that he would make all of the big decisions and that I would make all of the little decisions. So it has been, and I believe that the longevity of our marriage is due to the fact that in all these years there has not yet been one big decision to make ... In these autumnal years, I have often eased stress and fought depression by recalling the words of Jean-Baptiste Troisgros—the celebrated chef and bon vivant. He said: 'From thirty-five to forty-five women are old; but at forty-five the devil takes over and they become beautiful, splendid, maternal, proud. The acidities are gone and in their place reigns calm. These women are worth going out to find and because of them some men never grow old.'"
End of Chapter Eight.
RACHEL. Superlative! Imagine you being able to organize my endless prattle.
ROBERT. It was easy, actually.
RACHEL. That damned quote worries me.

ROBERT. Why?
RACHEL. It's not the truth.

(*ROBERT laughs.*)

RACHEL. What?
ROBERT. Nothing. You've reminded me of a dandy old Saroyan line: "Now that I've found the truth, I'm looking for something better."
RACHEL. Let's take it out. It seems embarrassing all at once.
ROBERT. As you wish.

(*HE makes the cut. THEY exchange a swift, could-mean-anything look.*)

ROBERT. Shall we go on or are you tired?
RACHEL. On, please, *on*.
ROBERT. With pleasure. "Chapter Nine." (*He looks up at her.*) Tough one.
RACHEL. (*Quietly.*) I know.
ROBERT. (*Continuing.*) "I have been most reluctant to write about the suicide of our son, Antonio, at the age of twenty-two, but the publicity surrounding this event has been so widespread that omission is impossible. Antonio, early in life, showed unmistakable musical talent, was playing the piano at age five and composing at seven. Vito supervised his musical education with great care and devotion. At sixteen, Tony won the Tchaikovsky competition in Moscow and shortly thereafter made his first concert tour. Although it was successful, he decided to switch to conducting which he had been secretly studying for some time. Vito managed to get him a few engagements and believed he was going to succeed. But Tony developed an obsession—"

(The CHIMES again. Puccini. Madame Butterfly. RACHEL responds.)

A NEW VITO'S VOICE. (*Gently and loving.*) Cara mia ...
ROBERT. Oh, *hell!*
VITO'S VOICE. You come up, please?
RACHEL. We're working.
VITO'S VOICE. One minute.
RACHEL. There's no such thing as one minute. Later.
VITO'S VOICE. (*Weakly.*) All right cara mia. All right. When you can. (*HIS voice fades away.*) Grazie a tutti. (*He clicks off.*)
ROBERT. (*Resumes reading.*) "But Tony developed an obsession—partially caused by the constant comparisons with his father—and for three years he vacillated back and forth from playing to conducting several times—"

(RACHEL puts her hand over her eyes.)

ROBERT. "—until he suffered a breakdown, recovered, resumed his career as a conductor—but then, believing he was ordained to live the rest of his life in the shadow of his father, he quietly put an end to it."

(RACHEL is weeping softly. ROBERT gets her a glass of water.)

RACHEL. Thank you.

(HE takes her hand and holds it for a time. The CHIMES. Pagliacci. RACHEL answers.)

RACHEL. Yes?

ERIC'S VOICE. I'm sorry, Signora, but Dr. Delmajian is here.
RACHEL. Send him right up to The Maestro's room and tell The Maestro that the doctor's on his way.
ERIC'S VOICE. Very well.

(RACHEL clicks off.)

ROBERT. Really nothing serious, is it?
RACHEL. No. He simply wants more attention than he's been getting.
ROBERT. He's quite a hypochondriac, isn't he?
RACHEL. He's not a hypochondriac—he just *thinks* he is.

(ROBERT laughs. RACHEL goes to the fireplace and tends to the fire, expertly.)

ROBERT. I suppose it all began the day Iris moved out.
RACHEL. *I* didn't ask her to.
ROBERT. I know—but she was mortified.
RACHEL. But isn't the main thing getting his book finished?
ROBERT. Well, they're doing that.
RACHEL. Are they?
ROBERT. She *says* they are. I had dinner with her last night.
RACHEL. Oh? Why?
ROBERT. *(Smiling.)* Nosey.
RACHEL. So am I. Where are they?
ROBERT. Nowhere near where we are.

(THEY shake hands.)

RACHEL. How much more do *we* have to do?

ROBERT. That depends on you. It's two more chapters—or three if we decide to tell this last piece.

RACHEL. I'd like to, except for two things.

ROBERT. Which two things?

RACHEL. Well, I don't want to malign Iris—and I don't know yet how it's all going to come out.

ROBERT. *I* do.

RACHEL. Oh? Tell me.

ROBERT. They'll finish theirs. We'll finish ours. She'll go back to Little, Brown in Boston. I'll go back to the Island and Mr. and Mrs. Maestro will go on as before.

RACHEL. What makes you so certain?

(*From above an eruption of loud ANGRY VOICES—a short screamer—four lines only—punctuated by a door SLAM and the sound of Someone coming quickly and heavily downstairs.*)

ROBERT. Where were we?

RACHEL. I asked you what made you so sure of your scenario.

ROBERT. Well. In this past year—I've come to know him—and you. So I understand his pattern.

RACHEL. *Do* you?

ROBERT. (*Gently.*) Rachel—how'd you like to take a crack at the last part now?

RACHEL. Now?

ROBERT. Let me try to steer you. (*HE sets up his laptop computer and switches on the tiny microcassette recorder.*) Oh—before you mention Iris, the reader's going to want to know why you condoned all these infidelities across the years. After all, there's such a thing as being *too* civilized.

RACHEL. Well, if the reader paid attention to the first part—then he/she would know that I knew the sort of man I was marrying. He'd been, all his life, a charmer, a ladies' man, a Lothario— why would I believe he was going to change overnight? In fact, I was surprised it didn't happen sooner.

ROBERT. When did it?

RACHEL. Not for almost a year. Then he went to Milan to conduct four performances at La Scala.

(*ROBERT is taking it down.*)

RACHEL. The Hungarian leading soprano—who shall remain nameless—Magda Verta—M-A-G-D-A— was a well-known wild one. In those days, I handled our business affairs. When the bills from the Hotel Mona Lisa arrived, I checked them, of course, and noticed each morning *two* breakfasts. How he could have been so careless I can't imagine. He was home by then. I fought myself for a day, lost, and confronted him. What do you think he said?

ROBERT. No idea.

RACHEL. (*Imitating Vito.*) "I was *hungry!*"

ROBERT. Hot dog!

RACHEL. What?

ROBERT. *What* a chapter finish! (*HE looks up at the ceiling and smiles.*) It's hard to be sore at him, isn't it?

RACHEL. I'm not. Just now I have the most enormous sympathy for him. He's a man with too great an appetite for life. He tries to get more out of life that there is *in* it. He knows he's in the final act of his play—resents it, wants his youth again, or a reasonable facsimile—needs to prove himself to himself. I weep for him.

ROBERT. But surely you don't think there's any future for him and Iris?

RACHEL. He's not looking for a future. He's looking for a past ... *His* trouble is that his wife understands him. (*SHE looks off, sadly*.) And I sympathize because I live with the same fears. Anxieties. Dreads. Is it almost over? Is it over? Was it a success? What have I missed?

ROBERT. Isn't it curious that someone as sensitive and intelligent as you can't see that—

(*HIS voice trails off. THEY exchange the longest possible look—perhaps half a minute.*
Then ROBERT puts down his notebook and his pen, turns off the recorder, and gets up. HE moves to her and stands for a moment, looking down at her. Now HE takes her head, gently, into his hands. HE leans down and kisses her, sweetly, long, and well.
VITO comes in, distraught. HE looks at them, but preoccupied as he is with his own exacerbation, does not see them.
ROBERT steps back. HE and RACHEL exchange a puzzled look.
VITO goes to the bar tray, gets himself a glass of Perrier and takes seven pills, all different. He wears black silk pajamas [acquired in Ceylon] a luxurious brocaded robe [from Barcelona] and velvet monogrammed slippers [Paris: John Lobb, Ltd.].)

VITO. When you will finish?
RACHEL. (*With a shrug.*) —half an hour? (*To Robert.*) Is that about right, Bobby?
VITO. Don' call it "Bobby!"
RACHEL. Why not?
VITO. What you mean half an hour?
RACHEL. We're tired. We've been at it all day.
VITO. I don' mean today—finish today! I mean when do you finish your goddam stupido book?

RACHEL. When do you finish *your* goddam stupido book?

VITO. We are finish already. Now. Ha! (*On the last word, HE gives them a powerful Neapolitan forearm salute.*)

RACHEL. Congratulations. I don't believe it. Do you, Bobby?

VITO. Don' call it "Bobby."

RACHEL. Why not?

ERIC'S VOICE. Miss Peabody is here, Signora.

RACHEL. Thank you. (*SHE calls out.*) Come in, Iris!

(*IRIS comes in.*)

VITO. We are finished, isn't it?

(*HE flashes his eyes at her desperately, as a signal. SHE is confused.*)

VITO. The book! Finished! Yes!

IRIS. No.

VITO. (*Hitting himself in the head.*) Madonna!

RACHEL. (*To Iris.*) How are you, dear?

IRIS. Frantic. And you being sweet to me doesn't help at all.

RACHEL. Bobby—

VITO. (*Almost to himself.*) Don' call it "Bobby."

RACHEL. —would you mind terribly if we called it a day?

ROBERT. Not in the least. It's been a grand one, hasn't it?

RACHEL. The best. Shall we leave the young people to themselves?

ROBERT. By all means.

(*They start out. ROBERT stops and kisses Iris, briefly.
VITO watches—then thinks, thinks.*)

ROBERT. See y'.
IRIS. Sure.

(*RACHEL touches Iris's shoulder and goes.*)

ROBERT. So long, Maestro.
VITO. (*Absently.*) Goodbye, Bobby.
ROBERT. Don' call it "Bobby!" (*HE starts out.*)
VITO. (*Coming to.*) Hey! Wait!

(*ROBERT stops.*)

VITO. Didn't I—before—see you—when I came in from up—before—you was kissing with my wife?
ROBERT. *ME?!* Are you *mad?* How would I—? Why would—? Are you well?
VITO. No—I'm sorry—maybe too much of medicines he puts me—that idiota doctor—make me many crazy dreams. I apologize. Scusi.

(*HE offers his hand. ROBERT studies it uncertainly for a
   moment—then, reluctantly, magnanimously, takes it.
   HE goes, closing the door.
VITO and IRIS are in each other's arms instantly. They
   silently exchange affection, vows, desires, passions, and
   love for a time.
Outside, two fire engines streak by—SIRENS wailing,
   BELLS clanging. Fire!
ROBERT comes back in, stops—then, realizing that
   THEY are in the clouds, comes into the room, retrieves
   his notebook and pen and recorder and computer. HE
   leaves again.*)

VITO and IRIS come out of it at last.)

VITO. What did he say?
IRIS. He didn't say. He *yelled*. He went berserk.
VITO. Berserk? Where is *that?*
IRIS. No—he—you know. Out of control. And he wouldn't take his ring back. I reminded him it was only a token—I never intended to marry him. But he wouldn't listen. He said I should throw it away—into the East River—or *he* would.
VITO. *Sell* it!
IRIS. Oh, I *couldn't.*
VITO. *I* will ... And the parents? More screamings?
IRIS. No.
VITO. No?
IRIS. They're wild about the idea. Proud of me and mad about you.
VITO. (*Confused.*) Why they are mad? You said—
IRIS. *Admire* you—adore you.
VITO. But what about the parents? Mother father?
IRIS. I *mean* the parents—my parents. *They* adore you.
VITO. Why?
IRIS. You know my father's an opera buff—and has been on The Boston Symphony Board for *ages*—and my mother hasn't missed a lunch at the Ritz and Symphony Hall on Friday afternoon in forty years.
VITO. Good. Is good.
IRIS. They think it's going to mean lots and lots of free tickets. I don't know why they care. They're obscenely rich.
VITO. Is the way. The more richer the people, the more want free passes. I take care. Also—they want—they come to rehearsals.
IRIS. They'll *die!*
VITO. Yes—well—we all got to die sometime!

IRIS. I mean they'll *love* it.
VITO. —and the brothers, sisters?
IRIS. I haven't any.
VITO. You are the only?
IRIS. Yes.
VITO. Too bad!
IRIS. Why?
VITO. —means you prob'ly spoil.
IRIS. I'm not as spoiled as *you* are, mister.
VITO. Maestro.
IRIS. Wait a second. Even after we're married—do I still have to go on calling you "Maestro?"
VITO. Ask Rachel. She knows everything.
IRIS. Does she know about our plans?
VITO. Not yet.
IRIS. Not *yet!?* What are you waiting for? What if she says no?
VITO. She will say what I tell her say. Has always been so. We go up now and work, no?
IRIS. No.
VITO. (*Astonished.*) No?
IRIS. No. I'll go upstairs and wait for you. You tell her.
VITO. (*Stalling.*) Tonight?
IRIS. *Now!* I can't leave here until I know where I stand. Is that clear?

(*VITO nods, rather sheepishly. IRIS gives him a sisterly peck on the cheek and leaves.*
VITO walks the last mile to the intercom.)

ERIC'S VOICE. Yes?
VITO. You tell the Signora I got to see her. Now.
ERIC'S VOICE. Of course, Maestro.

(*VITO goes to the bar tray. HE takes an old-fashioned glass
  and slowly fills it with Glenlivet scotch. HE looks at
  it, then drinks it in one long, slow draught.*
*Under his breath he rehearses what he will say to Rachel.
  As HE practices, RACHEL comes in.*)

RACHEL. Yes, sir.

(*VITO comes to her and puts his arms around her. A long,
  warm embrace that has everything in it but love. THEY
  are clinging to one another in the manner of two people
  going down with the ship.*
*Thus joined, HE walks HER around the room.
Finally:*)

VITO. Rachel. Please sit.
RACHEL. No. *You* please sit. (*SHE puts him into an easy chair.*)
VITO. I want to tell you some*thing.*
RACHEL. No need.
VITO. Huh?
RACHEL. It's in the air. I've been breathing it for weeks. Vito, dear. You want to tell me that we've had a remarkable marriage, that I've been an exemplary wife, and that you will always love me.

(*VITO seems about to speak, but SHE silences him with a palm.*)

RACHEL. But that there comes a time for a man—a desperate time—when he feels that if only life would give him one more chance, he could take it and have a truly happy ending. And this means breaking out of the trap—it means a kind of transfusion of youth—and a new outlook—and yes you love me—but in a different way.

You've earned the right. It's not too late. Look at Casals. At eighty-two, he married his nineteen-year-old pupil, Carmen, and they had thrilling years together. Look at Segovia—became a father at eighty-one and then had a little son to occupy him.

(*VITO tries again, but it is no use. SHE has taken command.*)

RACHEL We must remain friends always. More than friends. We must try to remember all our great times and years and places and happiness—and forget the mistakes and the mishaps. After all, our years are a near eternity. Everything wears out in time—machines, people, buildings—even a marriage. You want to remind me that we really have had the best of it, haven't we? It would probably be all downhill from now on. And anyway, you feel you're sort of falling apart. More and more ailments and symptoms and pains and why should you burden *me* with them? Let someone younger and stronger take over. You want to assure me that this, in the end, will doubtless turn out best for *me*. And, darling, I'm not sure I don't agree with everything you say. So of course you have your freedom if you want it. I've always given you everything you wanted if it was in my power to give it and I'm certainly not going to stop now. I've been to see a new lawyer—Edgar Halloran, a specialist—and he says that in view of the fact that *you* are leaving *me*, I am to dictate the terms of the settlement. (*As she continues SHE goes to the shelves and begins to look for something. The search takes HER, on the library steps, high up.*) They are as follows: From the day the decree becomes final, I want no money, no alimony, no share of your income from any source. However. This house and everything in it will be mine. Also the condo in Palm Beach. (*SHE finds the compact disc she has been searching for and comes down.*) Also my share of the royalties on any and all recordings, compact discs, cassettes, videocassettes, or films made *prior* to our divorce. (*SHE puts the compact disc onto the stereo and sets the volume control.*) Also the Rolls and the Bentley. The boat. Also all bank accounts, bonds, stocks, now jointly held.

VITO. (*Stands, stunned and in shock.*) But Holy Madre di Dio, Rachel! What *I* am suppose to live on?

RACHEL. (*Sweetly.*) Love, darling—*love!*

(*SHE touches the "play" button. MUSIC blares forth: The Wedding March from Lohengrin.*
SHE sails out in triumph. VITO stands frozen in shock. The MUSIC and LIGHTS fade fast.)

ACT II
Scene 3

A mellow evening. It is April again.
The dining room, entirely CANDLELIT. The two candelabra on the table are reinforced by six wall sconces. They combine to create a gentle, romantic ambience.
From the background, the soft SOUND of Vito's recording of Tchaikovsky's Romeo and Juliet with The Philadelphia Symphony Orchestra will continue throughout.
Seated at the table: VITO, IRIS, RACHEL and ROBERT. THEY are all in evening dress. Rachel, in her most dazzling Halston; Iris, a springtime sprite in her colorful Laura Ashley. Vito's dinner jacket, made by Johnson and Marié in Paris, is impeccable. The Van

Cleef and Arpels ruby and diamond cufflinks and studs, as well as the shirt, waistcoat, and tie are matchless. Robert looks pretty snazzy, too.
The key to the playing of this scene is: EVERYONE is charmingly tipsy.
Bruce and Eric are in pink jackets this time.
ERIC and BRUCE serve the crêpes suzette. First Vito, then the ladies, then Robert. The flame flickers up from each plate.

IRIS. Isn't this *festive!*
VITO. Cosa vuol dire, *festive?*
RACHEL. (*Italian.*) Festive.
VITO. Oh, sure! Sure!
RACHEL. (*To Iris.*) If you need an interpreter, Iris—I may be available.
VITO. No, no! No good idea!
RACHEL. As you wish.

(*Vito was the first to be served, so the FLAME on his plate flickers out.*)

VITO. Eric! Bruce!
ERIC. Yes—
BRUCE. —Maestro?
VITO. (*Adolescently truculent.*) Why everybody has the fire and not *me?*
ERIC. (*Looking at the plate.*) Oh—
BRUCE. —sorry—
ERIC. —Maestro.

(*THEY rush to replace the omission. EACH one brings a bottle. Bruce, the Curaçao; Eric the Cognac. THEY pour the spirits onto Vito's plate, overdoing it in their excitement. BRUCE lights it. A column of flame three feet high shoots into the air, startling EVERYONE as they jump away. VITO leaps to his feet and steps back.)*

RACHEL. (*Calmly.*) Eat it while it's hot, dear!

(*IRIS and ROBERT laugh. The flame subsides. VITO sits.*)

VITO. Grazie.

(*ERIC and BRUCE retire.*)

IRIS. Rachel—may I thank you again?
RACHEL. No need.
IRIS. There is for me. When you invited us—I can tell you now—I was frightened.
RACHEL. Of what?
IRIS. The situation. But you've made it so—uh—easy and simple and—well—*civilized*. So now—leaving tomorrow won't be so hard.
ROBERT. How long in San Francisco?
IRIS. Just a day and two nights.
RACHEL. Tokyo's a difficult flight. Try to sleep as much as you can.
IRIS. I will.
RACHEL. (*Making conversation.*) What about other plans? Everything settled?
IRIS. Well, not *everything*—but it's *not* going to be the Big Wedding my family was after.
ROBERT. Boston?
IRIS. Oh, yes.
VITO. Very good string section, The Boston. Silverstein. Concertmaster. (*HE kisses his fingertips.*) Magnifico!

IRIS. —But of course it won't be till we get back from Japan in June. Probably July or August.

ROBERT. August. I can't make it in July.

IRIS. —And then both books—pub date September sixth. I'm thrilled! Aren't all of you?

RACHEL. —Seems silly, in the circumstances, to still call mine MRS MAESTRO.

VITO. Change it!

IRIS. No, no—too late.

RACHEL. Is it, Bob?

ROBERT. I'm afraid so.

IRIS. (*To Vito.*) Is it all right to tell about the big stuff?

VITO. (*Generously.*) Oh, sure.

IRIS. (*Flushed with excitement.*) Well—it's not definite—my father had a little something to do with it. It's just that we may be taking over The Boston Symphony year after next.

VITO. *We?*

IRIS. We.

VITO. I see.

(*RACHEL and ROBERT exchange a meaningful look.*)

RACHEL. —And will that mean moving to Boston?

VITO. No!

IRIS. Yes.

VITO. Yes.

IRIS. —for a good part of the time, anyway.

ROBERT. (*Raises his glass of champagne.*) To Boston!

ALL. To Boston!

IRIS. Rachel—Vito says—

RACHEL. (*With a small smile.*) —Maestro.

IRIS. Vito says it's all right to ask you anything.

RACHEL. —Anything?

IRIS. —About arrangements and medicines and travel and routine and—

RACHEL. Of course.

IRIS. —and when he gets moody, for instance. Is it better to try and cheer him up or leave him alone?

RACHEL. —depends on what he's moody *about*.

IRIS. Uh-huh.

VITO. Hey! Don't talk about me like I'm not here! I *am* here.

IRIS. (*As before.*) —and about quarrels. Would you say it's better to win—or just give in?

RACHEL. Win.

VITO. Give in.

IRIS. I don't see how quarrels can be avoided. In fact, we're having one right now. A beaut. (*To Vito.*) Dear— would you please get that little blue box from my bag?

(*A long, pregnant and charged pause. IRIS eats. VITO glares at her. When SHE becomes aware of the fact that he has not moved, SHE looks up and adds:*)

IRIS. Now?

(*HE goes on glaring. RACHEL and ROBERT prepare for the big explosion.*
IRIS eats, happily. VITO glares. IRIS looks up at him. A long exchange.
Finally:)

VITO. (*Softly.*) —Little blue box?

IRIS. Please.

VITO. (*Getting up.*) Mi scusi. (*HE goes out.*)

RACHEL. (*Laughs and laughs.*) Iris—would you be interested in a position with Ringling Brothers, Barnum and Bailey?

ROBERT. (*To Iris.*) —and how's your Japanese coming along?

IRIS. (*Proudly.*) I know a hundred and sixty-six words and forty-four phrases. Food, tabamono; coffee, cohee; bathroom, obenjo; money, okana. I suppose I'll sound like a half-wit, but at least I'll be able to find a ladies' room and order a meal.

(*VITO returns with the little blue Tiffanys box, and sits.
ERIC is serving coffee.
BRUCE follows with a brandy tray.*)

IRIS. Now. Here it is. When I told Larry what had happened, he was—well, not happy. And I wanted to give him back his ring. And he wouldn't take it. As though it were some mad superstition or—I don't know. Anyway. He told me to throw it away. But I couldn't do that, could I? He said if I insisted or *sent* it back, *he'd* throw it away. Into The East River. So I don't know *what* to do. Any ideas?

VITO. *Sell* it!

IRIS. (*To Rachel and Robert.*) That's what we've been quarreling about. Selling it is his idea. (*SHE indicates Vito.*) But I'd feel dishonest doing a thing like that.

VITO. *Sell* it.

RACHEL. It's a dilemma, all right.

(*A pause.*)

ROBERT. *Sell* it!
IRIS. What?
ROBERT. To *me*.
IRIS. Why? What will *you* do with it?
VITO. Sell it?
ROBERT. Use it.

VITO. How much?

ROBERT. What it's worth. Easy to find out. From Tiffany's. Whatever *he* paid for it. And you can give the money to Save the Whales or whatever.

IRIS. Is it really for you, Bob? Honest?

ROBERT. Injun.

IRIS. Well then. (*SHE gets up and goes to Vito.*) May I have it, dear?

(*VITO hands her the little blue box. SHE moves around the table and takes it to Robert.*)

IRIS. Dear Bob. With my blessing.

ROBERT. No, Iris. I couldn't.

IRIS. It's the tiniest repayment. I owe you my whole new miraculous life.

ROBERT. How's that?

IRIS. Well—if you'd stayed on and finished the book— none of this would have happened.

ROBERT. I didn't do it deliberately.

IRIS. —But you *did* it. (*SHE presses the box into his hand and kisses him.*) All the best forever.

ROBERT. Thank you. (*HE takes the ring out of the box and looks at it.*) Wow! Damn glad I *didn't* have to buy it.

IRIS. Who's the lucky girl?

VITO. (*Beaming.*) Yes, *who?*

ROBERT. (*Gets up and moves around to Rachel.*) May I have your hand, please?

RACHEL. (*Extends her hand. To Iris and Vito.*) I suppose *I* am.

(*ROBERT places the ring on her finger, leans down, and kisses her.*

ERIC, *holding the coffee tray, is transfixed, as is BRUCE, with his brandy tray. IRIS and VITO are similarly frozen in shock.)*

IRIS. (*Suddenly breaking the freeze.*) My GOD!!

(*VITO, with one of his characteristic uncontrollable nervous spasms, is propelled to his feet in the manner of a missile. As HE does so, he knocks the tray out of Bruce's hands—it goes flying into the air. In an attempt to retrieve it, BRUCE slams into ERIC, who drops his tray and, trying to catch it, bumps VITO, who loses his balance and falls, sprawling, onto the table. Watch those candelabra, for God's sake!*
EVERYONE in the room goes to work with dispatch, repairing the damage. There is a good deal of confusion and interference, direction and criticism. But at length, all is done.)

VITO. Rachel! You have make me the gladdest man in whole university.
IRIS. Universe.
VITO. Thank you. Two times—when you marry me and when you say you will marry again. I thank you! (*HE kisses Rachel.*) I thank you. (*HE shakes Robert's hand.*) And I thank *you*. (*Explaining.*) God. (*HE looks up to God.*) I think now of my father. (*HE crosses himself.*) And how he teach me all my life—he had teached me big lesson—whatever he do—I do the op*pos*ite. How you say op*pos*ite?
IRIS. Opposite.
VITO. Op*pos*ite. Thank you. When he was old—he was fall in love with a young pupil—she eighteen, nineteen— he want to marry with her—his wife, my mother, say no. The girl's mother and father—also no. God, poco poco—

And the priest, no no no—so he don't and that make my father—he cry every night the rest of his life—so he was my big lesson—whatever he do—I do the—
IRIS. Op*pos*ite.
VITO. *Opposite.* (*Suddenly.*)*AH! HAH!!!* (*THEY all look at him.*) Is everything change now. Now is no more you the Rolls *and* the Bentley. Is now *OR* the Rolls *OR* the Bentley! Is *you* the here and *me* the Palm Beach—or upside down. And the pictures? Is fifty-fifty-fifty.

(*HE looks at BRUCE and ERIC who are suddenly petrified.*)

RACHEL. No, no! They are a team—

(*VITO is puzzled. SHE explains.*)

RACHEL. —like the Juilliard String Quartet.

(*VITO, confused, counts them.*)

RACHEL. A team.
ROBERT. Like Laurel and Hardy.
VITO. (*Comprehending.*) Oh! Another fine mess?
IRIS. (*Taking charge.*) How about— (*SHE points to Rachel and Robert.*) —you take them for six months, and *we* for six months—and then let *them* decide.

(*VITO—the old Vito—swings on her in a fury.*)

VITO. Shaddop!

(*SHE is startled, frozen.*)

VITO. *Shaddop!*

(*SHE is transfixed. ALL freeze.*)

VITO. Is no good you boss boss boss. You take the charge. You break the balls. Got to be fifty-fifty-fifty. If no—then nothing.

(*There follows the longest silent pause in the history of the theatre. The group becomes a Madam Tussaud exhibition. Anything can happen. Finally, finally, finally:*)

IRIS. (*Sweetly.*) Of course, darling. Whatever you say.
VITO. (*Ballsy.*) I say: (*To Rachel.*) *You* take them six months and we take them six months. And then we let *them* decide. (*To Iris.*) O.K.?
IRIS. (*With a shrug and a smile.*) O.K.
BRUCE. Thank you, Miss.
ERIC. (*A whispered echo.*) Oh, thank you.
VITO. (*In full charge now.*) And the stocks—the bonds? Communist property!
IRIS. (*Correcting him.*) Community.
VITO. Communist community.
IRIS. Property.
VITO. Property.
RACHEL. Just a moment, please.
VITO. Everything fifty-fifty-fifty.
RACHEL. But I don't see—
VITO. The boat—me.
IRIS. I get seasick.
VITO. (*To Rachel.*) The boat—*you*.
ROBERT. No, thanks. *I* get seasick, too.
VITO. Bruce! Eric! *You* want the boat?
BRUCE. (*Politely.*) No, thank you, Maestro. My father used to say—

ERIC. "A boat is a prison with a chance of drowning."
VITO. We sell it!
ROBERT. Good.
VITO. (*Happily.*) So that takes care everything, no?
RACHEL. Everything but my agreement.
VITO. So! You want better put the lawyers everyones together and *they* take everything?
ROBERT. (*To Rachel.*) He's right, my darling. My father said things, too. He's a lawyer and he used to say—"Never kill a case by settling it." (*To Vito.*) We agree.
VITO. (*To Rachel.*) You getting a smart boy, Rachel ... so, settled? (*HE raises his glass as do the OTHERS and toasts passionately.*) To the future! To the youth! To the age! To the marriage! To the love! (*A pause, then passionately.*) To the communist property! Saluta!
ALL. Saluta!

(*THEY drink.*
Now a series of emotional embraces:
VITO and IRIS. ROBERT and RACHEL.
VITO and RACHEL. ROBERT and IRIS.
IRIS and RACHEL. VITO and ROBERT.
VITO shakes hands with ERIC and BRUCE.
There are smiles and tears—but no further words.
VITO and IRIS leave, arms about each other, through the main door.
ROBERT and RACHEL go off in the opposite direction, into the fragrant garden—and disappear into the darkness.
BRUCE and ERIC stand for a long moment—BRUCE looking after Vito and Iris; ERIC after Rachel and Robert. Then, at the same moment, THEY turn and fly

into one another's arms. THEY embrace, powerfully, in an attempt to keep from drowning in the pools of love that have been left behind by the four adventurers.)

THE END

Author's Note

The following is the text for the offstage argument (ACT II, Scene 1) between VITO and RACHEL. It is strongly suggested that the entire dialogue be pre-recorded, then edited and modulated in volume to fit the onstage action. It is not necessary for the audience to hear the entire argument.

VITO. (*Offstage.*) You crazy? You crazy. I get you one doctor. Some kind good doctor for crazy. (*In Italian.*) È tanto che lo penso. Sei malata nella testa. Non ti comporti come una donna—come una moglie. Sei pazza. (*In English.*) You bring this little son of a bitch—this bastard—this son of a bastard—you bring him here in my house—he live in my house. What do you do with him? Sure, you say you writing a book with him. What book? Why? You crazy? Who wants your book? What have you got to say? You got nothing to say. Everything to say, I will say. It is one story—not two stories. I will tell the story. (*In Italian.*) Buttalo fuori! (*In English.*) You throw him out! (*In Italian.*) Se non lo butti fuori, lo butto fuori io. (*In English.*) You don't throw him out, I throw him out. (*In Italian.*) Forse vi butto fuori tutti e due. (*In English.*) This is my house. How you got the nerve—how you got the chutzpah. You have someone live in my house and you don't tell me. I call the police. No, no, lawyers—I call lawyers, they will see. You want to give me back my heart trouble? You want to give me back my atrial fibrillations. That's what you want. No, I don't lose so easy—I give you some atrial fibrillation. I don't act like some fool. (*In Italian.*) Mi vuol far becco? Mi vuol mettere le corna? (*In English.*) You are foolish—you are a foolish fool. You forget you are no more young. This young boy he is not for you. I am getting my sickness again. Is your fault. You got no rights. Why you do this to me? You woman—you bad woman! You bitch—yes, bitch. You behave to me in this way after all I do for you all my life. Shaddop, shaddop.

RACHEL. (*From off.*) If you want to discuss this matter seriously and sensibly and quietly, Vito, I'm prepared to do so. But if you are going to shout, I'm going to leave. (*SHE shouts.*) Did you hear me? I won't have any shouting. We are supposed to be two intelligent, mature and sensitive people. There is nothing more important in life than the ability to see it all from the other person's point of view. (*In Italian.*) E non voglio più sentir parlare di "casa tua." Capito? (*In English.*) This is not *your* house, it is *our* house—no, come to think of it, it is not our house, it is *my* house. This house is owned by the Pro-Musica Corporation, of which I am the president. I didn't want to be, but you and those lawyers of yours and those fancy accountants insisted upon it. So as it turns out, I am the president and you work for me. And I would strongly advise you to behave yourself. (*SHE shouts.*) And don't shout. Stop shouting. Do you hear? And now I have a few questions. I would like to ask you. Who went off on a long tour and left me behind to fend for myself? You. You. Who has systematically gone off on one peccadillo after another and expected me simply to turn the other cheek? You, my dear maestro, you. And who continually got us into financial straits over and over again? You, and you. And who always got us out? I and I. So I'll have none of this holier than thou attitude—you must stop behaving like a nineteenth century man—like an eighteenth century man—like a seventeenth century man—like your ideal—your Casanova. No, no, don't deny it, he is your hero—he has always been your hero. You envy him—you try to outdo him. No, you are quite wrong, there is nothing between young Robert and me, other than a splendid professional relationship. And if you could've behaved with him sensibly and reasonably, your bloody damn book would be finished by now and we would not be having all this ridiculous trouble with Little, Brown and Company. So, I think we better stop all this and go downstairs and resume my life, such as it is. I intend to be a good sport and I advise you to do so as well. Is that clear? Now stop it. (*SHE shouts at the top of her lungs.*) I said stop shouting!

COSTUME PLOT GEVA THEATRE

Rachel:
I-1 (April)

Dress - rayon jersey wrap style
Belt - rope style w/gold buckle & tassels
Shoes - suede w/rosettes; low heel
Hose
Jewelry: necklace; bracelets - 3; earrings; Rings - 1 gold wedding

I-2 (May)

Hose - same
Long coat - silk
Top - chemise silk
Pants - silk, lounge cut
Head scarf - matches coat
Shoes - low heel
Jewelry: necklace ; earrings; rings - same

I-3 (August)

Chemise
Blouse
Skirt
Scarf
Head wrap - turban style
Shoes - low heels
Hose - same
Jewelry: earrings; scarf buckle ; rings - same

II-1 (October)

Shirt/dress - long, silk
Leggings
Scarf - long, silk
Shoes - flats

Hose - same
Jewelry: earrings; watch; rings - same

II-2 (December)

Hose - same
3 pc. pants set
Belt - cloth
Shoes - flats
Jewelry: Necklace; earrings; rings - same

II-3 (April)

Eve. gown - long velvet
Wrap - sheer chiffon (silk)
Shoes
Hose - same
Jewelry: earrings; hair clip; ring - 1, gold
Hair - fluffed, with hair clip on right side

IRIS
I-2 (May)

Hose
2 pc suit - w/ self belt
Hat
Portfolio case
Blouse
Tie
Shoes - heels
Glasses
Jewelry: Watch; ring - small diamond engagement ring; earrings
Hair - up

I-3 (August)

Strike: watch
Dress - linen

Shoes - sling back & open toe
Hose -same
Jewelry: Necklace - beads; bracelets - 2 plastic; earrings
Hair - down

II-1 (October)

Dress
Coat
Hat
Gloves
Jewelry: Earrings
Hose - same
Hair - up

II-2 (December)

Purse - small
Blouse -
Hat - envelope style
Cape - wool
Skirt - w/self belt
Tights - (worn over hose)
1/2 Boots suede
Jewelry: Earrings; necklace
Hair - up

II-3 (April)

Dress - silk taffeta
Shoes - heels
Hose - same
Purse - clutch
Jewelry: Earrings; necklace & bracelet
Hair bow - matches dress
Hair - pulled back, low. Hair bow attached.

BRUCE & ERIC
I-1 (April)

Jacket #1 - beige
Bow Tie #1 - beige
Pants - black
Shirt - white formal w/front pleats, wing collar, black studs
Shoes - black tie
Sox - black

I-2 (May)

Same
I-2 to I-3 Scene change
Strike: Beige jacket, beige bow tie
Add: Yellow Jacket (#2)
Yellow bow tie (#2)

I-3 (August)

Same (Yellow)

II-1 (October)

Strike: Jacket # 2 (yellow)
Bow tie # 2 (yellow)
Add: Blue Jacket (#1)
Blue bow tie (#1)

II-1 to II-1 Scene change

Strike: Blue jacket (#1)
Blue bow tie (#1)
Add: Yellow Jacket (#2)
Yellow bow tie (#2)

II-2 (December)

Same (yellow)

II-2 to II-3 Scene change
Strike Yellow jacket (#2)
Yellow bow tie (#2)
Add: Pink jacket (#3)
Pink bow tie (#3)

II-3

Same (pink)

ROBERT
I-1 (April)

Sports jacket
Tie
Shirt
Pants
Belt
Socks
Shoes
Jewelry: Watch
Glasses

II-1 (October)

Vest
Shirt
Pants
Shoe slip-on
Socks
Belt
Jewelry: Watch - same
Glasses - same

II-2 (December)

Shirt - same
Sweater - pull-over

Pants - corduroy
Shoes - same
Socks - same
Jewelry: watch -same
Glasses - same

II-3 (April)

Shirt - white formal w/front pleats, turn down collar
Tux jacket - black w/ shawl collar
Tux pants - black
Cummerbund - black
Bow tie- black
Shoes - black tie
Socks - black
Accessories: watch - same; shirt studs - black; glasses - same

VITO
I-1 (April)

Kimono - silk
Shirt
Pants - black (not formal)
Shoes - black slip-on
Socks - black, thin
Jewelry: 2 rings - gold filigree & diamond, onyx & diamond; neck chain - gold
Glasses

I-2 (May)

Sports Jacket
Pocket handkerchief
Slacks
Shirt
Socks - same
Shoes - slip-on

Jewelry: same
Glasses - same
Belt
Underdress: I-3 shirt

I-3 (August)

2 pc suit - linen
Shirt - (underdressed)
Tie
Pocket handkerchief
Shoes - slip-on
Socks - thin
Jewelry: same; tie clip
Belt

II-1 (October)

Suspenders
2 pc. suit - double-breasted
Shirt
Tie
Pocket handkerchief
Overcoat - wool
Hat - fedora
Shoes - slip-on
Socks
Jewelry: same; Watch; neck chain - same

II-2 (December)

Pajamas
Dressing gown
Slippers
Jewelry: same
Socks - same
Strike: watch
Underdress: II-3 black formal pants

II-3 (April)

Suspenders
Pants - black formal (underdressed)
Tux jacket - double breasted black w/white gardenia in breast pocket
Bow tie - rigged to shirt
Shirt - White formal wing collar (rigged CB closure)
Pocket handkerchief
Shoes - black patent slip-on
Socks - same
Jewelry: same

PROPERTY LIST GEVA THEATRE

<u>ACT I, scene 1:</u>
FURNITURE: sofa, sofa table, end table, chair, end table, music stand, desk chair.
PROPS: Music score on stand, laptop computer, briefcase with:
> sm. notepad, microcassette recorder, extra pencils and pens, papers;

manuscript and pencil, manuscript, dictionary, date book, hand mirror, bar with:
> gin decanter, vermouth decanter, vodka (Absolut), scotch (Glenlivet), wine bottle, little Perrier bottles (3 or 4), 2 martini shakers, ice bucket with ice and tongs; corkscrew, glasses (4 martini, 4 wine, 4 highball), twists and olives; baton, lollipop,

first tea tray with:
> teapot, cream, sugar, lemon;

second tea tray with:
> 3 cups & saucers, tea strainer, 1 teaspoon.

<u>ACT I, scene 2:</u>
FURNITURE: sofa, sofa table, end table, 2 chairs, end table, bar, bench seat, library steps
PROPS: Gucci envelope, manila folder with:
> comptroller's estimates and list of writers;

bar set-up (same as scene 1)

<u>ACT I, scene 3:</u>
FURNITURE: bar, dining table with 3 chairs (4th chair not at table
PROPS: Fruit bowl in center of table; 3 place settings on table with:

placemat, napkin, silverware, underliner plate, bread plate, wine glass, water glass, bell (by Rachel's place)

cart, wine bottle, biscuit tray with tongs and biscuits; 3 jellied madrilène in bowls on plates; 1 tray to clear madrilène, 1 tray with 3 lobster salads (2 real, 1 fake) & serving utensil as needed; 1 tray with:

>champagne bucket, Dom Perignon wrapped in towel (in bucket), 3 flute glasses;

2 extra flute glasses, 1 tray with:

>3 bowls of lemon souffle,

fresh plate of lobster salad for Vito, coffee tray with:

>coffee pot, cream & sugar, 3 cups & saucers;

Gucci envelope with steno pad and pencil

ACT II, scene 1:

FURNITURE: Same as I, 1

PROPS: Microcassette recorder, laptop computer, briefcase, Rachel's notepad, Robert's notepad & pen, Bar - same with a corked wine bottle & an open Perrier bottle; first tea tray with:

>3 cups & saucers, teapot, tea strainer, cream, sugar, 2 cloth napkins

second tea tray same as above EXCEPT:

NO teapot, NO napkins, with lemon, with 4 cups & saucers (instead of 3)

2 trays with tea sandwiches on napkins, long-handled dustpan and broom, 1 cup & saucer (to replace one that is thrown)

ACT II, scene 2:

FURNITURE: Same as I, 2

PROPS: Microcassette recorder, laptop computer, briefcase with: same as before plus folder with chapters 6,7,9 paper-clipped individually, chapter 8 Rachel's story

paper-clipped, Rachel's notepad, bar same as before
with: Perrier water bottles, bottle opener; disc in jacket,
fireplace accessories, 2 pill bottles with pills, handful of
loose pills

ACT II, scene 3:
FURNITURE: same as I, 3 EXCEPT: 4 chairs at table
PROPS: 4 table settings with:
> placemat, napkin, underliner plate, 1 fork, 1 spoon,

bell (by Rachel's place), rolling cart, 6 champagne glasses, 4 water glasses, tray with:
> empty Dom Perignon bottle wrapped in towel, champagne bucket

tray with crêpes, 4 crêpe plates, 2 bottles flambé alcohol, 2 long lighters, coffee tray with:
> 4 cups & saucers, cream, sugar, coffee pot

brandy tray with:
> 4 glasses, 1 bottle brandy

Tiffany box (and ring), bar: same as before with open wine bottle

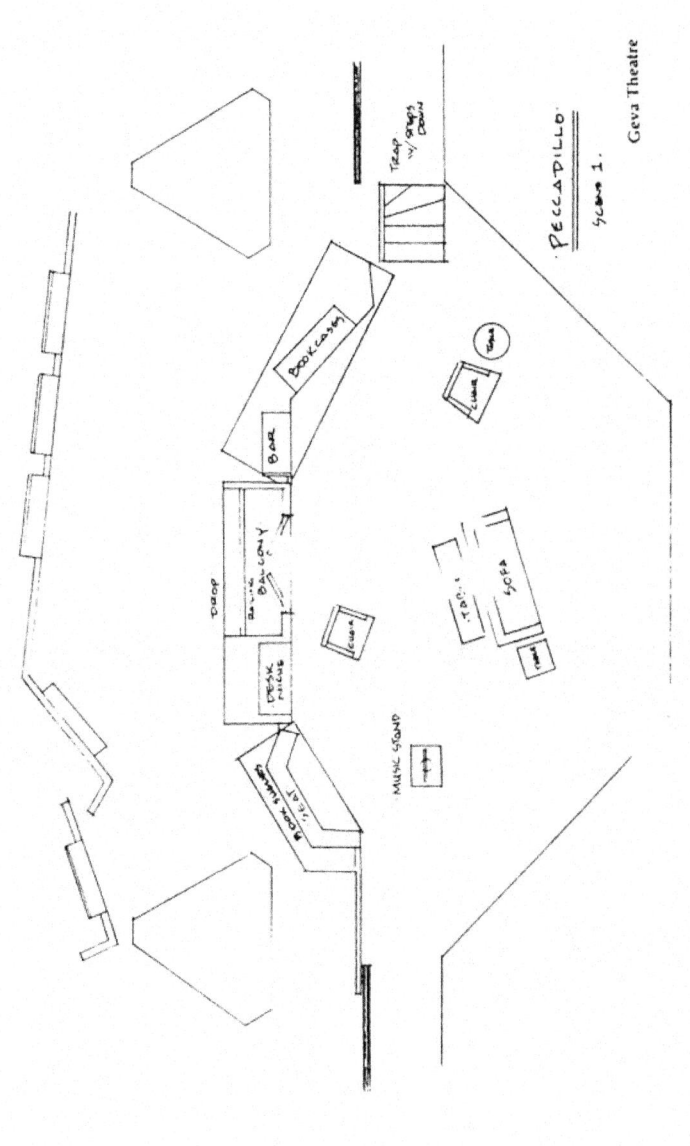

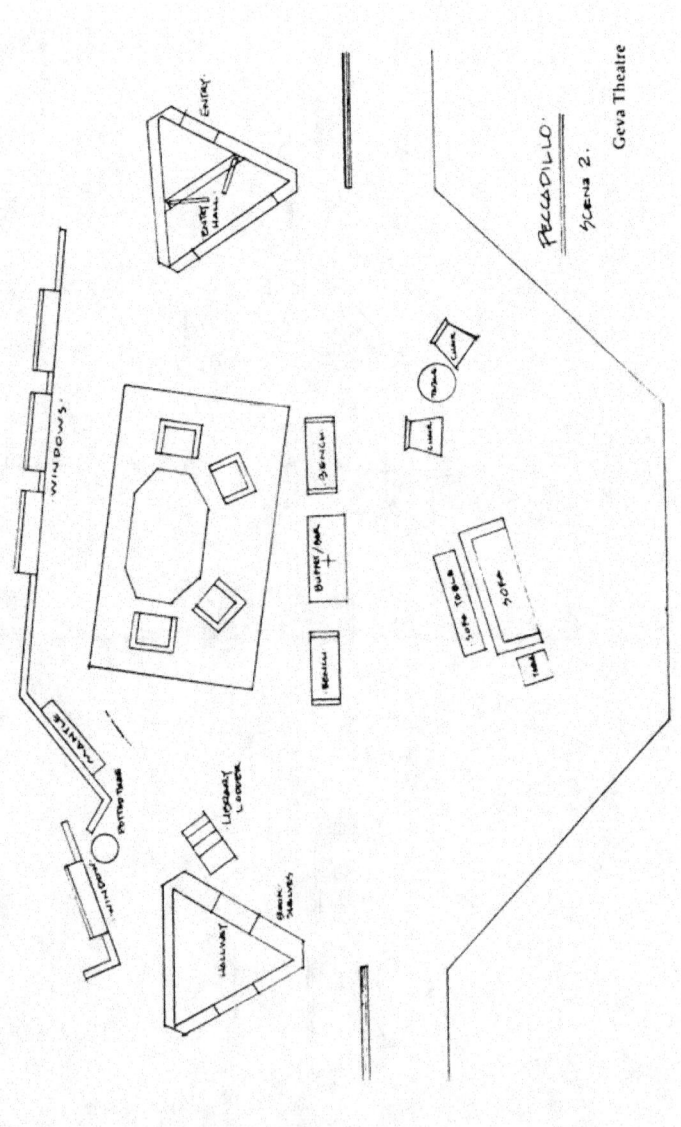

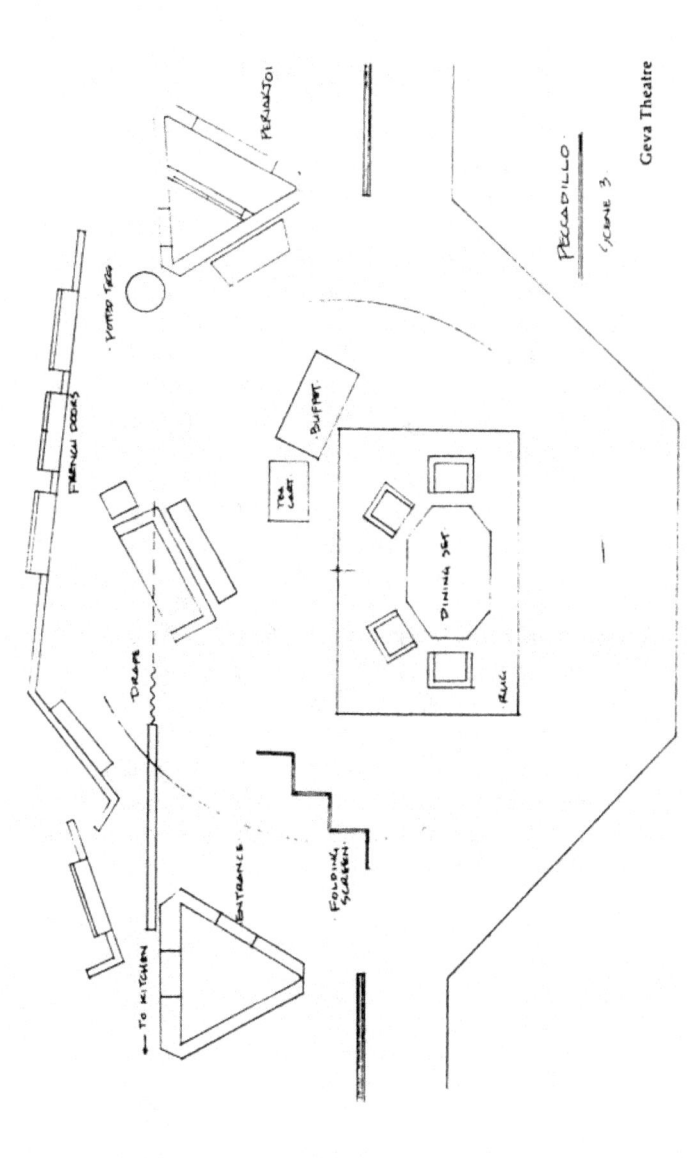

Garson Kanin

Playwright, novelist, screenwriter, actor, director, producer, musician and librettist—Garson Kanin has had great success in many aspects of the performing arts. He is the author of *Born Yesterday, A Gift of Time,** the memoir *Tracy & Hepburn*, the novella *Do Re Mi* (later adapted for the musical stage and directed by Mr Kanin) and director of *The Diary of Anne Frank* and *Funny Girl* on stage and *My Favorite Wife, Bachelor Mother* and *Tom, Dick and Harry* on film. With Carol Reed, he co-directed the Academy Award-winning World War II documentary *The True Glory*. With his late wife, Ruth Gordon, he wrote the classic screenplays *A Double Life, Adam's Rib, Pat & Mike*, and *The Marrying Kind*. His many books include *Remembering Mr. Maugham, Hollywood, Smash, Moviola, A Thousand Summers,* and *It Takes a Long Time To Become Young*. A member of the Theater Hall of Fame and a recipient of the William Inge Award for Lifetime Achievement in the American Theatre, Mr. Kanin is on the council of the Dramatists Guild and President of the Authors League of America.

---

*Also handled by Samuel French, Inc. Consult our *Basic Catalogue* for details.

**Also by
Garson Kanin...**

Born Yesterday

A Gift of Time

Remembering Mr. Maugham

Please visit our website **samuelfrench.com** for complete descriptions and licensing information.

OTHER TITLES AVAILABLE FROM SAMUEL FRENCH

A GIFT OF TIME

Garson Kanin

Drama / 5m, 5f, extras / 4 sets

An American editor resigns his post and moves to France with his wife and two children to spend his time in writing important books. But all too shortly he learns that he is dying of an inoperable cancer, and forthwith determines to live every day, hour, and minute to the fullest: life is a gift of time. Gradually he begins to feel the pain and physical consequences of his affliction. Unfortunately, he even becomes immunized to morphine. He decides, therefore, to bear the pain and the debilities so long as his faculties remain. At that point, with his wife holding him tightly and murmuring, "I love you. Please die," he cuts his wrists and ends the agony. In the Broadway roles, Henry Fonda played the dying husband, and Olivia de Havilland, his wife.

"The affirmation of the dignity of man in the face of the remorseless enemy - mortality. Will shake you and move you. Shining tenderness. Celebrates with tenderness and humor the gifts of love and understanding that make life worth living."
– *New York Times*

"Done with remarkable taste and intelligence, and results in an emotional experience of unrelenting candor."
– *New York Post*

"It held the first night audience in a relentless and awesome grip."
– *New York Daily News*

"A strong and honest drama."
– *New York Journal-American*

SAMUELFRENCH.COM

OTHER TITLES AVAILABLE FROM SAMUEL FRENCH

REMEMBERING MR. MAUGHAM

Garson Kanin

Memoir / 2m

Remembering Mr. Maugham is an intimate glimpse into the life of W. Somerset Maugham – one of the most brilliant, prolific and secretive writers of the 20th century. This graceful two-character, one-act play adapted by Garson Kanin from his memoir is a treasure trove of private conversations, amusing anecdotes and candid recollections of his beloved friend and confidant. Through decades of friendship, Kanin and Maugham poignantly reminisce about life, art and the unconquerable human spirit.

SAMUELFRENCH.COM